Race and Culture in Education

Issues arising from the
Swann Committee Report

Edited by T.S. Chivers

NFER-NELSON

Published by The NFER-NELSON Publishing Company Ltd.,
Darville House, 2 Oxford Road East,
Windsor, Berkshire SL4 1DF, England

First Published 1987
Reprinted 1988, 1989
© 1987. Copyright for individual chapters remains with the
individual copyright holders.

Typeset by First Page Ltd., Watford.
Printed in Great Britain by
Antony Rowe Ltd, Chippenham, Wiltshire

ISBN 0 7005 1152 0
Code 8287 02 1

Contents

Contributors

Terry Chivers, who is convenor of the British Sociological Association's Race and Ethnic Relations Study Group, is Principal Lecturer in Sociology at Sunderland Polytechnic.

Carlton Duncan, who was born in the West Indies, is now headmaster of George Dixon Comprehensive School in Birmingham. He has extensive experience of public service on bodies concerned with race relations, and was a member of the Swann Committee. Currently he is an assessor in county court cases involving race relations under the 1976 Race Relations Act. Of his extensive publications on race and education, his *Multicultural Education: Towards Good Practice* (with R.K. Arora) was published in 1986.

Patricia Keel was Senior Community Language Co-ordinator for the City of Newcastle upon Tyne. Her research on multicultural education has been co-ordinated at Sunderland Polytechnic. She is now at the London Borough of Ealing's Centre for Reading and Language Development.

James Lynch is Dean of the Faculty of Education at Sunderland Polytechnic. Professor Lynch has published extensively on multicultural education; his *Multicultural Education: Principles and Practice* was published in 1986.

Winifred Mould is an Advisory Teacher, Equality of Opportunity, North Tyneside Education Authority. Her M.Ed. on multicultural education was obtained at Newcastle University in 1986.

John Rex, who was born in South Africa, is Research Professor and Associate Director at the Centre for Research in Ethnic Relations, Warwick University. He is among the best-known writers in the academic world on race and ethnic relations. His Occasional Paper 3, *The Concept of a Multicultural Society*, was published by the Centre in 1985.

Wendy Robertson, who is Senior Lecturer in Education at Sunderland Polytechnic, has been teaching on multicultural education and publishing research over a number of years.

Barry Troyna is Reader in Education at Sunderland Polytechnic, and was formerly Senior Research Fellow at the Centre for Research in Ethnic Relations at Warwick University. Of his various writings, *Racism, Education and the State* (with J. Williams) was published in 1986.

Gajendra Verma, who is Reader in Education at the University of Manchester, has an extensive record of educational research and publication. He served on the Swann Committee.

Editor's Note

NAME is now termed the National Antiracist Movement in Education; the acronym, before 1985, stood for National Association for Multicultural Education.

Introduction

T.S.Chivers

This book is about race and culture in education; its concern is with what has come to be known as 'multicultural education'. The reader might next expect several lines of definition to explain that term. However, no such lines appear – and the reader is entitled to know why.

The term 'multicultural education' has entered the educational jargon in recent years as the British education system has sought to come to grips with the fact of a society composed of a range of minorities. In particular, ethnic minorities had entered Britain from the New Commonwealth and Pakistan after the Second World War, and their offspring were becoming pupils in increasing numbers from the late 1950s.

Initial policy with immigrants was to assimilate these minorities into the British way of life. However, any notion of complete absorption was soon proved to be unrealistic, and a phase of integration followed, in which the minorities were to retain their distinctive ethnicities. So far as schools were concerned, that meant that education would need to take account of the ethnic minorities; but exactly *how* was not really clarified. Rather what occurred was a realization that some kind of adaptation was required to respond to the sheer number of pupils from the minority ethnic groups: Taylor with Hegarty (1985) put it in terms of 'the pressing sense [that] the aims of education deserve revision'. This marked the birth of the concept of multicultural education, and during the 1960s and 1970s discussion about the form that multicultural education should take in the schools passed through further phases, traced by Swann (1985) and Taylor with

Hegarty (1985). The accounts are informative and throw light on the different and conflicting approaches.

Even so, one may still ask: what is multicultural education? Here the books are of little help; the ink, as it were, has run dry. One cannot help but wonder whether the popularity of the term was anything more than a weak response to the visibility of numerous children of the minorities in Britain. In other words, because there were, in some towns, many such children, it followed that something called 'multicultural education' (or similar) should appear as a curricular item: a single slot somewhere on the weekly timetable. This occurred in some schools.

Probably, however, the reason for the silence in the matter of definition is more subtle. To read the accounts of the course of discussions about multicultural education is to realize that one is attending to a debate about the form of that definition. Certainly, at the intellectual level, there is a search for the appropriate words to explain the meaning of the term. But below this is a far more important debate, taking the form of a social struggle on behalf of the ethnic minorities to bring an end to the pain and fear of racist experience. Because the minorities have learned that racism is pervasive within British society, the educational change which they seek is equally far-reaching. If education is impossible to define in one slick sentence, then so is multicultural education. One is talking about the education system itself; the curriculum as a whole; the orientation of pupils and staff; and the outlooks brought in from outside the school and how the school responds to them. Multicultural education, then, has to do with a way of life, one that is attempting to wrestle with social and political change and having considerable implications for the British education system.

None of the contributors to this book has directly tackled the issue of definition, outlined above. They certainly address the debate itself, however, in that they discuss the context in which that definition shall be developed. Thus Rex develops his discussion of multicultural education within the context of two concepts: 'equality of opportunity' and 'anti-racist education'. These two are held to relate to each other, that anti-racist education is necessary in order to produce equality of opportunity. He then spells out the steps required for the realization of these two concepts in the schools. In his view, the discussion about underachievement in the

Swann Report serves only to divert attention from the real issues indicated by the two concepts. In other words, underachievement might be described as a symptom of the absence of multicultural education.

For Lynch, the context has to do with prejudice reduction in schools, and he sets out a series of principles necessary for a genuine reduction. His aim is to devise a parameter within which prejudice can be realistically tackled. This is as close as Lynch comes to anti-racist education, a topic of much concern to other contributors (see Keel, Troyna and Duncan). In this connection, Keel talks of the injustices, distortions and imbalances brought about in the education system by racial prejudice, and she proceeds to draw attention to those people who 'believe that education needs to address itself to combating racism'. Troyna believes that anti-racist policies in the schools fail to be dealt with in the Swann Report, whereas Duncan integrates the idea into sweeping curricular reform, in line with the Swann argument. Duncan's special contribution is to show just how much that curricular reform is needed.

Several of the contributors mention Swann in terms of mutual support. They use the Committee's arguments to back up their points while, at the same time, supporting the Committee's case. Thus both Mould and Verma see the Report as a lever with which to open up multicultural activity. Similarly, Rex cites the Report as a reasonable agenda for reform: 'It certainly gives me a charter for the kind of anti-racist reform of the educational system which I wish to bring about.'

Not so for Troyna. He seeks to expose the political context by which Rampton/Swann was subtly diverted from finding out what was wrong with the educational system. Instead of investigating schools, attention was turned on to the perceived needs of pupils of West Indian origin. By this, he means the needs as perceived by the white politicians and professionals concerned with giving direction to the Committee. Thereby was the problem shifted from the school on to the minorities themselves. The consequences were far-reaching. Thus there is no study in the Report of the generation of racism within the school; hence too the focus on underachievement, no doubt spurred on by fears of black unrest.

The issue of underachievement is the focus of Verma's contribution. In this respect, the Report is found wanting. Verma, like

Troyna, points to the lack of any systematic analysis of the causes; Swann's conclusion that racism is an important influence is never substantiated analytically; rather the case which is made is very confusing. Pupils of West Indian origin do less well at school than the average for pupils as a whole. Some south Asian minorities seem to perform at around average yet the Bangladeshi children seem especially to underachieve. The Report supplies no explanation based on research, so that the reader is left with a puzzle.

While Verma and Troyna are close in their concern for the technical inadequacies of the Report, Troyna's central dissatisfaction is with the Report's shortcomings of policy. No case for promoting the minorities' cultures within the school system is made and no way forward against racism at school is ever developed. Small wonder, since the Committee never considered the operation of racism within the school. The Report has missed the point!

It is possible to identify several debates within the above discussion.

1. Does the Swann Report provide an agenda for educational reform, or is the Report ultimately irrelevant because it does not explain how change within the school could take place?
2. What, if any, is the relation of underachievement to multicultural education?
3. What is the best context for the definition of multicultural education: anti-racist education, promotion of minority cultures within the school, curriculum change affecting all subjects – or what?
4. Is the real problem white racism? Swann says it is, but the evidence presented in the Report is shaky. Moreover, how should racism be tackled: at the level of individual prejudice or at the institutional level where sets of accepted behaviours support racist stereotypes, however unknowingly?

It is common to meet with dispute in the debate, and these arguments are reflected among the present contributors. In addition to the different approaches to multicultural education and the different interpretations of Swann is a third issue: the strategies for change. To promote equality of opportunity and anti-racist education, Rex and Troyna want political education in schools. Rex argues that this would provide a foundation for the development of anti-racism. Troyna favours a thorough-going investigation of institutional racism as a basis for the development of anti-racist educational policies. One can discern something of what this institutional racism is by considering Mould's and Duncan's evidence of racism among pupils. There is also the unperceived racism among teachers (see Duncan and Robertson). Too often, it seems, school staff see neither their own racism nor that of the pupils.

Robertson's work is principally about this problem. As she says, only by a good deal of self-awareness may a teacher avoid unconsciously passing on a culture imbued with racist elements. Without such awareness, teachers may reproduce racism, even though they personally condemn it. Then there are the teachers who prefer not to consider racism. To all these groups, Robertson suggests possible ways forward.

Among the various policies discussed by Lynch is staff development. He outlines the principles which would need to be followed for this to lead on to prejudice reduction. Mould's focus is the role of the local education authority, and, within that, the role of the advisory teacher. How should the LEA help to promote multicultural education? She sets out practical answers. What should the advisory teacher do? She has many suggestions (see Appendix I to her contribution).

Keel supplies an answer which deserves the most careful consideration. Her action research model, operated by staff on a participative, non-directional basis, provides at least one way whereby racism can be tackled. She even advocates the use of this model for the curriculum change urged by Swann. In her view, this kind of activity is best carried out by teachers themselves. None the less, Keel is honest enough to acknowledge the shortcomings of her model. Only a minority of staff in her study became deeply involved, while, at the other extreme, some teachers remained disengaged from the entire project. It seems clear that there is no one right way forward. Keel's method is no doubt useful but it would need the support of Mould's, and of Robertson's, suggestions too, and who knows how many others?

Taken as a whole, the contributions shed light on the essential components of the debate and action taking place in multicultural and anti-racist education in the north-east of England. Three of the contributors supply a good deal of information about the local

scene. Thus Mould and Robertson discuss local issues, while Keel
devotes a whole chapter to the regional context. The relevance of
the locale to the Swann argument should not be overlooked. Parts
of the north-east are virtually exclusively white communities, yet
racism abounds and hence the need for multicultural education.

The contributions themselves derive from a conference on
'Multicultural Education after Swann', held in March 1986.
Organized by the British Sociological Association Race and Ethnic
Relations study group, the conference was sited at Sunderland
Polytechnic where the Faculty of Education has emerged as a
centre for the study of, and research into, multicultural and
anti-racist education.

References

SWANN REPORT, GREAT BRITAIN, DEPARTMENT OF EDUCATION AND
   SCIENCE (1985). *Committee of Inquiry into the Education of
   Children from Ethnic Minority Groups. Education for All,*
   Cmnd 9453. London: HMSO.
TAYLOR, M.J. with HEGARTY, S. (1985). *The Best of Both Worlds...?
   A Review of Research into the Education of Pupils of South
   Asian Origin.* Windsor: NFER-NELSON.

1 Multiculturalism, Anti-Racism and Equality of Opportunity in the Swann Report

John Rex

The greatest danger with regard to multiculturalism is not whether it will be implemented in schools, but what will be implemented in its name. Neither the goal of equality of opportunity nor that of anti-racism logically and simply lead to multiculturalism; in fact, multiculturalism may well be their antithesis. If we insist that minority children in schools should have something different but do not ask the question of whether that which is different is also not inferior, we shall gain great support for multiculturalism precisely from those who think that these minority children *are* inferior.

Nineteen years ago I took part in the UNESCO experts' meeting on the nature of racism and race prejudice. At that meeting some of our members wanted to put in a reference at the head of our statement to the 'rights to be different'. We deliberately voted against any such inclusion because, as we saw it, if it were inserted, it would be used by every oppressive regime and apartheid government to justify racial inequality. President Botha, surely, would support the blacks' right to be different!

British education is not simply about the transmission of moral values and skills, it is about certificates and about selection. Any educational policy, therefore, which prevents groups of children from getting certificates, from getting selected, is a betrayal of those children, however wholesome that which stands in the way may be in and of itself. It seems to me possible that multicultural education may play this role.

There is of course an inherent difficulty in our educational system. It is certificate-oriented but, in the nature of the case, only, say, 20 per cent are going to get the worthwhile certificates. This poses the problem of what should be provided for the 80 per cent. There are, not surprisingly, many who believe that this is *the* educational issue.

Those who believe in equality of opportunity and anti-racism of course believe *both* that minority group children should have equal opportunity and that it matters what sort of education is given to those who don't succeed in terms of certificates. Some, however, have identified the cause of multiculturalism with, and solely with, the education of the 80 per cent. Thus one leading member of an education committee, when challenged to show that multiculturalism would have a bad effect on formal educational standards measured in terms of certificates, replied 'I don't care if it does; I'm concerned with the 80 per cent who don't get such certificates'.

Alternatively, others have agreed that multicultural education *should* be confined to the low-status uncertificated parts of the syllabus. It can be taught in primary schools and in the lower streams, but should not affect the certificated high-status subjects which can continue as before. Thus competition and selection are thought of as going on, undisturbed by multiculturalism at lower levels.

In order to arrive at an understanding of how we can achieve *both* equality of opportunity and a multicultural syllabus, I think it is necessary that we should look *both* at the implications of equality of opportunity for minority children and at the ideal of a multicultural society and the ways in which it might be brought into being. I believe that if we do this, then we will be able to develop a concept of education which also fulfils a third ideal: it will be inherently anti-racist.

Equality of Opportunity

Some time ago I developed a check-list of items necessary to guarantee equality of opportunity to the minority child in school. I quote here the version of this list which I submitted in a paper to the Swann Committee:

1. Instruction of non-English-speaking children in their own language at the point of their entry into the system not in

order to segregate them permanently, but that they should not be prevented at an early stage from learning to learn by a situation of linguistic and cultural shock.

2. Instruction in the mother tongue, so that children should not have to pay the price of being unable to communicate with their parents for any success which they may have in education.

3. The early introduction to English as a second language, with adequate arrangements to ensure that the time spent on acquiring English does not prevent progress in normal school subjects.

4. Second-stage English instruction to ensure that children are given not merely minimal English, but sufficient command of the language to enable them to cope with study at whatever level they are otherwise capable of reaching.

5. The inclusion in the syllabus of subject-matter relating to their own culture, so that they are not deprived of their own inheritance, and can see that it has recognition within the curriculum and within the value system of British society (this requirement not being met by paternalistic teaching at a low level, which could have the effect of denigrating rather than strengthening minority cultures).

6. The teaching of minority languages, history and culture up to the highest level and not merely in the low-status and uncertificated parts of the syllabus, so that these subjects have equality of status with, say, French language, literature and history.

7. The elimination from the syllabus in all subjects of all those elements derived from an earlier historical period in which the culture of minorities is denigrated and a positive emphasis in the syllabus on the histories and cultures of their countries as an important part of the education of all children.

8. A positive commitment on the part of the school to the elimination of racism through the syllabus as a whole, through specific teaching against racism and through school practices which treat racism as a disciplinary offence.

9. The employment of qualified schoolteachers from the minority groups in all subjects and a guarantee that they will be promoted on merit.

Obviously such a programme would by itself go far in fulfilling the ideals of multiculturalism and anti-racism as well as achieving equality of opportunity. Item 5 is the one which overlaps most with multiculturalism. It should be noted here, however, that the bracketed qualification is all-important and that it might be added that such teaching is best provided by part- or full-time teachers drawn from minority groups themselves. Item 8 covers anti-racism which is important not simply in its own right, but as a means to the end of equality of opportunity.

One point which, perhaps, should have been made is left out because I regarded it as obvious. This is that all selection processes whereby children are assigned to classes, streams or bands should be based upon academic performance and not upon teachers' assessment of behaviour. I would now want to add this explicity in the light of the findings of the Eggleston Report (1984). Perhaps I should add, though, that allocations to classes on grounds of behaviour might well be argued for by teachers as a sign of their multicultural sensitivity. This is precisely the danger of multiculturalism to which I have drawn attention. It is on the basis of stereotypes that children are differentially treated, and those stereotypes are as likely to be derogatory or patronizing as not. We do best for minority children's equality of opportunity by sticking to formal academic criteria.

One objection to giving equality of opportunity the prominence which I have given it is that such equality does not exist for other children, particularly working-class children. Of this, I would say that it in part rests upon a mistaken belief that what we are talking about is equality of outcome. It should be clear that we are not and that for the foreseeable future, and in comprehensive systems as well as three-stream systems, there will be more rewards for some than for others. We can't wish such a system away and, if it does come and we believe in equal opportunity, we should be concerned to ensure that all children have an equal chance of unequal rewards.

More important is the notion that working-class children do not enjoy equality of opportunity within the present system. This is true. All that I can say about it is that someone should write a check-list of items necessary to overcome the barriers that presently stand in their way. If the success of minority children in winning their rights here were to lead to working-class demands, so far as I am concerned, so much the better. The present position is that minority children are doubly disadvantaged. They are from minorities and they are usually working class. Their minimum demand would be that they be allowed the same opportunities as working class children. For all children to have equality of opportunity, however, it would be necessary to review the system from the point of view of the minorities and of the native working class.

The programme which I have outlined, however, may be held to fall short of what is necessary for education for a multicultural society. Thus many will argue that a multicultural education programme applies not only to the minority children and the schools where their presence is evident, but the middle-class, largely white suburban school as well. For that reason, it will indeed be necessary to outline and give the rationale for a multicultural programme which includes such schools, but before we do, it is necessary to insist that a genuine multicultural programme cannot, and must not, leave out the needs of the minority child in the minority school.

Too often the notion of 'multicultural education for all' or 'education for a multicultural society' has simply left out any consideration of rendering efficient services like E2L or mother tongue teaching which are at present abysmally inadequate.

Education for a Multicultural Society

The notion that Britain is a multicultural or multisocial society is asserted both widely and glibly. Such assertions, perhaps, mean little in practice apart from a generalized feeling of well-being on the part of those who assert them. If we are serious about the notion of multiculturalism, we must specify the precise and limited sense in which we use the term.

One meaning which does not apply in the British case is the notion that somehow or other power in Britain is to be shared between the British majority and the Caribbean and southern

Asian minorities in the way in which it is shared, say, between the Walloons and the Flemish in Belgium, or between the French- and English-speaking sections of the population in Quebec. We do not expect these minorities to have equal numbers of seats in Parliament or even reserved seats in one of the Houses of Parliament. We do not expect that their language will rank equally with English in government business or that they will have an equal share in civil service posts. Nor do we expect that they will have separate school systems. These are some of the aspects of a certain kind of plural society.

Still less do we expect or want the creation of another kind of plural society such as that which exists in its present form in South Africa in which multiculturalism is continually asserted but the segments are thought of as having unequal power. Here again, we must insist that multiculturalism is a dangerous notion unless it is coupled with some concept of equality of opportunity or equality between plural segments.

Finally, we should notice that any concept of multiculturalism which undermines the concept of equality of treatment in the public domain is unacceptable. The right of the individual to a vote, the right to equal treatment by the police, the right to form free trade unions and to engage in collective bargaining as well as the hard-won social rights of the welfare state constitute a common political culture which is not only part of the British tradition, but is supported by all minority groups. Any attempt to undermine this common system of rights and to replace it with a British equivalent of South Africa's Ministry of Bantu Affairs has to be opposed whether it comes in the name of pluralism or multiculturalism or in any other guise.

But if these more grandiose concepts of multiculturalism are rejected, what remains of the concept? Just this, I think: that in a society committed to equality of opportunity in all spheres of the public domain, it is recognized that there is also a private communal domain in which each community and ultimately each individual will choose his own way of life. This plural domain includes the regulation of sexual and family affairs and all matters concerned with religious or moral education. Tolerance of diversity in these respects is an achievement of our civilization as hard-won as the rights and liberties which guarantee equality of opportunity.

It is easy enough to say that such tolerance should exist; it is harder to acknowledge it in detail and in practice. Our society's values are individualist and we are likely to extend the notion of the rights of the individual to involve not merely his rights in the market-place and in the public forum, but also his or her right as against the family. Thus it is not surprising that feminists find it hard to accept the limitations on the freedom of women which Asian family and marriage systems impose. Many of them would call for a radical change in these systems, and in so doing, would do much to undermine the distinctive communal culture of Asian minorities.

The harshness of this clash of values occurs because we in the majority community seek to impose our values without really understanding what minority values are about. In fact, what the Asian minorities are seeking to assert is that there are some things which should not be treated as commodities and they are horrified at the crude marketing of sex which they see as an endemic part of our culture. Feminist values espoused by insensitive majority women appear to them only as a part of this larger package. Of course it is true that the translation of customs from sending society to the society of settlement means that those customs may be insensitively applied. But what matters is that changes in them should be brought about by members of the communities themselves. Anyone who knows and trusts Asian communities will know that members of these communities are themselves questioning and modifying their values on family matters, and that it is through their solutions that they will adapt to living in British society.

The issues which I have raised here are central ones when we consider what is happening in our schools. Schools are in part the instruments of the larger society in the public domain. They are concerned with the transmission of skills and the broad political values of our society. They are also concerned with the process of selection whereby individuals are allocated to different destinies in life. As such they are likely to be corrosive of communal values of any kind. Yet they also assume responsibility for moral education, and what we have attempted to do in this area is to foster values of neighbourliness and solidarity without which a purely individualist society would become simply a war of all against all. The sources of these values have been found in Christianity, in the experience of family and community and in the class solidarity of working people.

Immigrant communities view our schools with some ambivalence. On the one hand, they see them as having a high instrumental value. To get on in the world of the market-place and the public domain, one needs education and certificates. Schools are necessary because they provide these. On the other hand, the school may seem to be saying 'You must abandon all your own group values when you come here and you must be assimilated', or alternatively, 'So far as moral values are concerned you must learn the Christian and British ones which we teach'.

In response to these latter demands immigrant minority parents develop quite specific demands. They want their children to have instruction in the mother tongue and in the ways of behaving and thinking that go with the mother tongue. They want their children to continue to respect the values of their own community, and they want them to preserve appropriate standards of dress, decorum, food and behaviour even if they conflict with what is on offer in the school.

At first, this is a fight which has to be fought by individual families, but sooner or later religious organizations appear, whether Pentecostalist churches among the West Indians or mosques and temples among the Pakistanis and Indians, and these organizations set up alternative bases to the school from which the moral training of the young can be organized. Nowhere is this more evident than in Muslim communities. In Birmingham, for example, where there are some 40 mosques, thousands of children receive instruction each evening after school in the mother tongue, in Arabic, in the Quran and in the way of life which the Quran teaches.

What are the implications of this for the schools? They are, I believe, twofold. On the one hand, they must themselves provide for, and relate themselves to, the provision which is being made for the moral education of minority children. On the other hand, they must ensure that all children learn tolerance of cultural diversity. The process of moral education in schools becomes a pluralist one in which all children can see their own community's values represented, even if it exists in a stronger form outside. At the same time, all children should learn to respect the diverse views of others, even if their particular school happens to have – as white suburban schools often have – a monocultural population. All children should have the opportunity of learning about their own community values and all should learn something about the values of others.

A more radical view is taken by some Muslims, as it has been taken for a long time by Roman Catholics. This is that if schools have to fulfil both a selective and a morally educational function, control should not lie with the selectors but with those who stand for communal and religious values. Inevitably we shall see Muslim schools. It will then be for Muslim parents and teachers to ensure that the maintenance of moral cohesion is not bought at the price of abandoning material success.

One of the reasons why the case for Muslim schools is strong is that schools have made such a poor job of moral education and education in community and religious values. Usually taught by white British teachers, the context of such teaching is often quite inadequate, involving a paternalistic caricature of the culture about which it claims to be teaching. Clearly, if the schools are to do a better job, they must find some way of involving community teachers in the educational process either by appointing more minority teachers full-time or part-time or relating themselves to what goes on in supplementary schools. Merely to tell existing schools and existing staff to 'be more multicultural' is not enough. What we are likely to get in this way is tokenism at its worst. It can be argued that, if this is all the schools can offer, they would do better to leave the job to the minority communities themselves.

Yet when that is said there clearly is a problem if the perpetuation of minority cultures exists only on the margins of society. The argument for bringing it into the schools is that in so far as we are able to do this effectively, then minority cultures will have a recognized place within our social system and our culture. And if they have such a place, they should have it not merely in schools where there are large numbers of minority children, but in all schools and for all children.

From Multiculturalism to Anti-racism

It will be seen from what I have said that both the ideal of equality of opportunity and that of multiculturalism leads on to the notion of anti-racist education. Equality of opportunity leads to it because there is no way in which such equality of opportunity can be guaranteed if a group of children or their cultural background are the subject of racial abuse and if those who operate the selection process show a racial bias. Multiculturalism leads to it because it becomes apparent that the main aim of a multicultural syllabus is to encourage respect for minority children and their cultures. None the less, it is important that the concept of anti-racism should be developed in its own right.

Anti-racism is an issue which must be posed in relation to the behaviour of teachers and pupils and as a matter of concern in the curriculum.

So far as behaviour is concerned, a policy of anti-racism in schools requires an explicit statement that racial harassment and abuse will be punished and that appropriate punishment will be imposed whenever such behaviour occurs. It also involves raising the level of awareness of racism among teachers, so that they take note of incidents which they may previously have regarded as not unusual or inevitable.

One particular and more central aspect of teachers' 'racism' is the operation of a racial bias in selection processes. When students are selectively assigned to classes, bands and streams, criteria for assignment should be as objective as possible. Clearly, there may be some margin of discretion to allow for special cases, but any case in which such discretion leads to the downgrading of a minority child should be the object of special investigation. This is perhaps the key area in schools where racial bias operates through stereotypes. Such stereotypes need to be brought into the open and criticized if equality of opportunity is to be attained, and the commitment to multiculturalism should not be used in an attempt to justify special and different treatment for minority children. The report by Eggleston *et al.* (1984) shows how systematically minority children have suffered in this matter, by being assigned to lower streams and classes.

So far as the curriculum is concerned, there are two matters which require consideration. The first is the 'deracialization' of the old curriculum. The second is the explicit appearance of anti-racism as part of the syllabus.

There are many who say that the emphasis here should be on an anti-racist approach of the whole syllabus. The danger, however, is that, unless the details of such an approach are made explicit, claiming to do everything will actually lead to doing nothing. What is required is the development of studies of particular syllabuses and teaching practices and a statement by heads to their staffs that such an anti-racist goal is being set.

A commitment of this kind will clearly have greater impact if anti-racism itself is a part of the syllabus. I believe personally that this should be part of the political education which all children should receive. Generally education in politics should be so planned as to ensure that children are exposed to a variety of views. This is essential in a free society which wishes to avoid indoctrination. But there are a very small number of ideas, which should be presented as the view of all legitimate parties. Anti-racism is one of them.

One of the difficulties about developing an anti-racist policy in schools is that one cannot assume that those who will be called in to carry it out will themselves be free of racism. For this reason, it is necessary that local education authorities should make their position clear and then see to it that teachers undergo special professional training, so that they become aware of the dangers of racism. Colleges concerned with the training of teachers must also make this issue central and explicit in training. Of course there is a problem, in that local authorities and colleges of education are themselves not wholly free of racism, but the goal of anti-racism has been made explicit in the Swann Report and elsewhere, and it is now possible to begin the difficult task of pulling ourselves up by our own moral and political boot-straps.

The Swann Report

We are now in a position to approach the Swann Report critically. We shall have to ask how well it understands and proposes to deal with each of the problems of equality of opportunity, multiculturalism and anti-racism. My own view of equality of opportunity as the most central concept is set out in the check-list of items, above. On multiculturalism my view is that it is a matter for which responsibility has to be shared between the schools and the communities themselves, so far as the education of minority children is concerned; but that when it comes to the education of the white suburban child, the whole question of multiculturalism becomes merged with that of anti-racism. Anti-racism as a policy must be seen as central to a policy of equality of opportunity and requires a quite explicit commitment on the part of all those who train or employ teachers, so that it becomes a part of the ethos of society and part of the professionalism of education.

Swann did not start from that position and could not because its starting-point was in Rampton, and Rampton had been instructed to give priority in his work to the underachievement of West Indian children, even though he was also commissioned to study the whole problem of the education of ethnic minority children. The result was that the Rampton problematic which Swann inherited was that of West Indian underachievement and whether this was due to – or perhaps to be blamed on – the schools and the teachers on the one hand, or the West Indian family and community on the other.

The Swann Report tries to get away from this somewhat childish problematic – and partially succeeds in doing so. It begins with two perceptive chapters on the nature of a multicultural society and on the nature of racism and only then goes on to pick up the argument about underachievement. The chapter on the multicultural society seems to me to be excellent and to accord entirely with my own view of a common culture in the public domain characterized by equality of opportunity and a variety of cultural forms in the private domain. This should provide an excellent basis for the discussion of multicultural education. The chapter on racism is also surprisingly clear and should provide the basis for the development of anti-racist policies in schools. The role of teachers' stereotypes, of the climate of racism outside the school and of racist attacks and racist name-calling are all well discussed, and should serve to suggest specific arrangements to combat racism in schools.

Unfortunately, the argument of the Report as it develops in chapter 3, on underachievement, comes to hinge not on the Committee's concepts of multiculturalism and anti-racism, but on its analysis of underachievement.

The argument goes like this: low IQ is not a significant factor in West Indian underachievement (mercifully, the research contribution of Professor Mackintosh and Dr Marcie Taylor buried that interpretation). Underachievement is associated with socio-economic status in the case of all children. West Indians do worse than other children even when class is taken into account, but what is to be expected is that they suffer an extra element of deprivation: 'A substantial part of ethnic minority underachievement, where it occurs, is...the result of social prejudice and discrimination on the part of society at large, bearing on ethnic minority homes and families and hence, *indirectly,* on children. Some discrimination, however, bears directly on children within the educational system. Research evidence on this is obscure and confusing, but none the less,

> It will be evident that society is faced with a dual problem: eradicating the discriminatory attitudes of the White majority on the one hand and, on the other, evolving an educational system which ensures that all pupils achieve their full potential.
> In the short-term, the first of these problems is a matter for the Law, the Government, Housing Authorities, Employers' Unions, the CRE and many others. But in the long-run we believe that it is a matter for the schools to bring about this change of attitudes amongst coming generations.
> The second problem is specifically one for the educational system. (Swann Report, p.90)

What the Swann Committee calls 'Education for All' is 'an attempt simultaneously to change attitudes amongst the White majority and to develop a pattern of education that enables all pupils to give of their best'. In other words, multicultural education must aim at changing white attitudes and overcoming black underachievement at the same time.

The term 'multicultural education' is rejected because it 'has encouraged schools and LEA's in "all-white" areas to believe that the issues involved are of no concern to them' and the term 'education for all' chosen because it 'reflects the responsibility which we feel that those concerned with education share in laying the foundations of the kind of pluralist society which we envisaged'.

It is unfortunate that the Swann Committee adopted the rather vacuous title *Education for All* for the programme which it presents and that it offered it as a means of overcoming the discrimination leading to underachievement. None the less, there is much in what they have to say about its meaning which suggests that they do keep the egalitarian and anti-racist goals emphasized here firmly in mind. Among the points which it emphasizes are the following:

1. Education should 'help pupils to understand the world in which they live and the interdependence of individuals, groups and nations'.

2. 'The richness of cultural variety in Britain should be appreciated and integrated in educational curricula at all levels.'

3. Education is seen 'as having a major role to play in countering the racism which still persists in Britain today'.

4. *Education for All* therefore seeks 'to identify and to remove those practices and procedures which work, directly and intentionally or indirectly and unintentionally, against pupils from any ethnic group'.

5. The 'syllabus recognizing the multi-ethnic character of Britain' should 'be used in all schools'.

6. 'It is also essential that the education system caters for any specific needs which (ethnic minority) children may experience in order to offer them the equality of opportunity which (has been) relocated.'

7. The concept of education for all raises immediate and obvious issues in the field of language teaching and religious education but there is a need to re-evaluate the curricula on the basis of the following criteria:

    (a) the variety of social, cultural and ethnic groups and a perspective of the world should be evident in visual, stories, conversation and information;

    (b) people from social, cultural and ethnic groups should be presented as individuals with every human attribute;

    (c) cultures should be sympathetically described in their own terms and not judged against some notion of 'ethnocentric' or 'Eurocentric' culture;

    (d) the curriculum should include accurate information on racial and cultural differences and similarities;

    (e) all children should be encouraged to see the cultural diversity of our society in a positive light;

(f)   the issue of racism at both institutional and individual level should be considered openly and efforts made to counter it.

8.   Political education should be an essential part of the syllabus. It should 'open pupils' minds to a full appreciation of the role which they as adults can and should play in shaping their futures'.

In learning how 'some long-established practices were originally developed to cater for a homogeneous population', children should also 'consider whether such practices are still appropriate to...change...British society today', or whether they are against the interests of minority groups.

Some views and attitudes are arguably unacceptable in our democracy: racism, suppression of opinion, exploitation of the defenceless ... Education which identifies the evils we must resist – and suggests how we may resist them – is quite proper and likely to command wide support. (Swann Report, p. 336)

In principle this is a very thoroughgoing agenda. It is one which Swann sees as being implemented through the initiative of the DES, the Inspectorate, the LEAs, multicultural advisers, headteachers, heads of department, examination boards, colleges of education and ordinary teachers.

It seems to me that this agenda does meet the needs to which I was trying to refer earlier. It emphasizes the notion of equality of opportunity; it does not base its concept of multiculturalism on a paternalistic and caricatured concept of minority cultures; and it targets racism both indirectly through a syllabus for all which treats minority culture with respect and directly through anti-racist teaching. It certainly gives me a charter for the kind of anti-racist reform of the education system which I wish to bring about.

I would hope that all those who wish to see an anti-racist educational system will take advantage of what Swann has offered. We are no longer talking about a situation in which a few idealists fighting against the mainstream are propagating a minority doctrine. Whatever local councillors or reactionary headteachers and others may think of the matter, we have the Swann Report on our side. It is up to us to see that its principles are fully implemented.

Reference

EGGLESTON, S.J. *et al.* (1984). *The Educational and Vocational Experiences of 15 – 18 year old People of Minority Ethnic Groups*. Department of Education, University of Keele.

2 The Swann Report and Ethnic Achievement: What Next?

Gajendra Verma

The Swann Report is the outcome of the Committee of Inquiry into the Education of Children from Ethnic Minority Groups. The Report, entitled *Education for All*, appeared in March 1985 (DES, 1985). In spite of this title, the main focus of the media coverage and comments from educationists has been on the question of achievement and underachievement of West Indian and Asian children in British schools. It may be argued that given the Committee of Inquiry's terms of reference, it is not surprising that commentators have responded by focusing on the issue of educational achievement/underachievement only. None the less, it is also true to say that the Report clearly points out that the question of achievement and underachievement is a complex one and that there is a wide variety of educational and social issues implicated in the education of all children in British society. In this article I have attempted to evaluate some of the main conclusions of the Report and indicate their implications for Britain today and tomorrow. Before this analysis, it might be appropriate to remind ourselves of the context of the Report.

In Britain, like many Western countries, the emerging 'pluralist' composition of society has been a matter of debate in the last two decades. This pluralism has arisen as a result of postwar migration to Britain. At the initial stages the educational system responded primarily in terms of equipping ethnic minority children to cope with life in society. The issue then began to shift away from pure survival to one of whether the structure of the educational system could offer those children the same chances of academic success as those enjoyed by the ethnic majority at large. Issues like educational needs and aspirations, achievement and underachievement of ethnic minority children started coming to the fore. By the early 1970s ethnic minority communities (effectively people from the New Commonwealth countries), teachers and some educationists started expressing their concern about the poor educational performance of such children within the system. Research, both large and small, conducted during this period also showed that ethnic minority children, particularly West Indians, were performing less well than their white peers. Studies also indicated that West Indian children were over-represented in schools for the educationally subnormal. The results of research into Asian children were contradictory and inconclusive – some showed that they were doing on a par with white children, while others suggested they were not doing as well as their white counterparts. However, the concern of ethnic minority groups was recognised by the Select Committee on Race Relations which reported in 1977.

The government felt unable to ignore the obvious fact that in a multi-ethnic society the population is composed of a number of distinct cultural, linguistic and religious groups which present a new and challenging reality for the educational system. It also legitimately requires an appropriate and fair response to all children. However, the government responded to public concern, particularly to the Select Committee on Race Relations, by setting up in 1977 a Committee of Inquiry into the Education of Children from Ethnic Minority Groups. It asked the Committee to look into the educational needs of children from all ethnic groups with priority given to children of West Indian origin. As a result, the Interim Report which appeared in 1981 was primarily concerned with children of West Indian origin. Given the terms of reference, the Committee also looked into the education of children from Chinese, Italian, Ukrainian and Vietnamese backgrounds as well as Liverpool blacks and the children of travellers; but the main thrust of the Inquiry was on children from West Indian and Indian sub-continent backgrounds. It must be pointed out that the Committee's appraisal of smaller ethnic groups was rather superficial.

Some Issues

In order to evaluate the broad conclusions of the Report, it might be useful to answer the following questions. First, is it true that some ethnic groups underachieve within the British educational system? Secondly, what criterion/criteria were used by the Committee to assess achievement/underachievement? Thirdly, what factors, according to the Report, contribute to underachievement if children from certain ethnic groups are underachieving? Fourthly, what can be done to help those children who are underachieving? It is easier to formulate questions than to extract answers from the Report. However, the Report is not explicit on most of the issues.

Returning to the first question, in general terms the Report says that West Indian children, on average, are underachieving in British schools and that Asian children, again on average, are performing on a par with their white counterparts. Such a generalized statement was highlighted by the media, and the readers might have been left with the assumption that all was rosy with children from Asian backgrounds. The weakness of the Report is that it has treated children from the Indian sub-continent and East Africa as a homogeneous group. The evidence obtained to draw such a conclusion has ignored the widely differing linguistic, social, religious and cultural traditions and experiences of the Asian sub-groups. The same might well be said of the West Indian groups. (This point will be taken up again.) Furthermore, it is not known what contribution particular privileged sub-groups (e.g. East African Asians) make to overall performance of what is crudely labelled as the Asian group. The report has drawn attention to one sub-group – the Bangladeshi – who are particularly disadvantaged and underachieving in schools. Our own research (Verma and Ashworth, 1986) showed that children of Pakistani origin in West Yorkshire are doing badly in schools. The Report has mentioned that the performance of children from Asian sub-groups is possibly subject to considerable variation. It has also acknowledged the complexity of the issues in the educative process and has asked the readers to exercise caution with regard to the evidence on which the conclusions are drawn. Yet the Report has given the impression that children of Asian origin are doing well within the British educational system. The

Committee should have made every effort to collect separate data for Asian sub-groups and from different parts of the country. Failure to do that is obviously a major weakness in the Report. The answer to the first question is based on so many qualifications that it can simply be suggested that some Asian children are performing well while others are not. To form the assumption that Asians are doing as well as their white peers is self-deception. A similar analysis can be given about the West Indian group.

The next question arises as to the criterion/criteria of under-achievement. In Britain it is primarily defined in terms of examination results, and such information is derived typically from CSE, O- and A-level results. Few would disagree that examination performance itself is too simplistic a measure of achievement. The Report has failed to provide any satisfactory answer to the question of what is meant by achievement. Educational achievement is not simply the fulfilment of intellectual potential as measured by performance in public examinations. Such indicators overlook the performance of a considerable part of the school population, particularly in the later stages of compulsory schooling.

One of the main sources of evidence in the Report to draw conclusions from came from the Department of Education and Science (DES). During 1981–82 it conducted a School Leavers' Survey to find out the number of CSE, O- and A-level examination successes under three categories: West Indian, Asian and others. Thus such categories of ethnicity have little relevance in explaining achievement and underachievement. It must be pointed out that ethnicity is not a permanent attribute of one's identity. Furthermore, the DES School Leavers' Survey failed to draw any distinction between ethnic minority children born in Britain and those born in the country of origin.

The Swann Report relied heavily on the evidence produced by the School Leavers' Survey. This had other obvious flaws. For example, it is fairly well known that the so-called 'East African' Asian groups have had greater exposure to Western influences educationally, socially and commercially and, therefore, are more privileged compared to other Asian sub-groups. A large majority of them came from urban backgrounds in Kenya and Uganda, whereas a high proportion of those originating from the Indian sub-continent are from rural areas. Thus it is evident that any data dealing with achievement of the Asian group is of questionable validity. The Report has acknowledged this and warns against the simplistic interpretation of achievement on the basis of currently available incomplete statistical evidence. Yet it presents the generalized conclusion in a way which seems to have misled readers.

As indicated earlier, the Report mentions the Bangladeshi group whose performance appeared substantially below that of other Asian sub-groups. This group was the last to arrive, has poor housing and is subject to much racial abuse and discrimination. The Report points out that Bangladeshi children are doing badly in school. It fails, however, to provide any satisfactory explanations as to why they underachieve in school. There is sufficient evidence from other reports and studies that racism in school and society at large affects adaptation of this group to life in British society. Assuming this to be true, it is inconceivable that other Asian groups are not affected by racism, both at school and in the wider society.

Besides the DES survey, other evidence utilized in the Report to ascertain educational performance of the main ethnic groups came from small-scale studies. The findings of such studies are susceptible to local factors and therefore cannot be directly compared with national patterns. Given the design of small-scale studies it is often difficult to have confidence in their findings. These points have been overlooked in the analysis of achievement/underachievement. Thus the DES research and many other studies are of limited value when one considers the area of measurement.

Another crucial issue overlooked by the Report is the fact that when differential performance is examined, the judgement is often based on the 'average' performance for the different groups. It rarely happens that researchers attempt to ascertain individual variations within a given group. For example, the fact that a set of scores show that group A's performance is inferior to that of group B does not mean that all the individuals in group A are performing badly. Our research (Verma and Ashworth, 1986) has shown that intra-ethnic differences are greater than inter-ethnic differences.

The third question posed at the outset is concerned with the factors contributing to underachievement of certain ethnic groups. The Report has put forward a number of explanations based on evidence (e.g. written and oral evidence, research studies and the previous literature). It has rightly rejected the simplistic notion that underachievement of the West Indians could be explained in terms of low IQ studies which matched the West Indian group with whites in terms of social class, difference in IQ turning out to be insignificant. It is fairly well established that IQ is not a significant concept in explaining human behaviour. Indeed, the chapter by Mackintosh in the Swann Report demolished IQ as an indicator by which educational achievement should be judged. The Report points out that socio-economic circumstances are closely associated with achievement for all children and, therefore, appear to contribute significantly to differences in achievement for all ethnic groups. It would seem difficult to refute this suggestion altogether since there is evidence in the literature that socio-economic circumstances have a bearing on the psychological make-up of an individual and consequently affect interpersonal relations, attitudes, motivation, self-esteem, and so on. Assuming that socio-economic circumstances affect performance of all ethnic groups, then performance of poor whites should also be affected, as is the case. The Report adds that West Indian families suffer extra deprivation because of racial prejudice in society at large.

The Report holds that stereotyped attitudes among teachers influence achievement, especially underachievement. It can be argued that if socio-economic circumstances, racial prejudice and discrimination in society at large and racism in the educational system contribute to underachievement, then all the Asian sub-groups must also underachieve. There is evidence to show that Asian children suffer from multiple disadvantages and encounter racial prejudice and discrimination to the same extent as West Indian children. But according to the Report, they do not underachieve with the exception of Bangladeshi children. The Report explains the differential performance in terms of tightly knit Asian families, positive parental attitudes towards education, and so on. If this explanation is accepted, then the Report has failed to explain the poor performance of Bangladeshi children or Pakistani children in West Yorkshire. Thus it is evident that the factors which contribute to underachievement are ill-understood and therefore, as an academic, I consider that there is a need for further research in this complex area of human behaviour. I do not believe, however, that such research is a necessary prelude to positive action. Quite enough is known *now* for such action to be initiated.

The final question is that, if certain groups are underachieving, what can be done to help them both within the school system and in the wider society? The Report does not provide a 'real' solution to the problems faced by ethnic minorities in British society. It acknowledges, however, that ethnic minorities have many difficulties and disadvantages to overcome before they can enjoy the same life-chances as their white peers in British society. The Report has recognized that biases in the educational system have contributed to the failure of ethnic minority children to achieve their full potential. It says that the educational system can perform its task by replacing the present monocultural with multicultural and anti-racist education which aims to cultivate equal respect for, and a sensitive understanding of, all cultures. The Report further argues that the danger of failing to address adequately the question of 'education for all' would provide a stimulus for certain ethnic groups to set up separate schools.

It is clear from the analysis of some of the main conclusions of the Report that the evidence offered is inconclusive and sometimes conflicting, and the explanations are provisional. This suggests that the issues relating to achievement and underachievement are both complex and ill-understood. None the less, the message from the Swann Report is clear: if all the children are to receive a good education, it is vital to overcome racism in all its forms, inside as well as outside the school. The means of overcoming racism, of course, are not easy to implement and many different manifestations of ignorance, hostility, misunderstanding and institutional inequality have to be tackled. Above all, it is essential that both structural (in society) and institutional (in school) changes must take place at the same time. The existence of racism outside the school is of enormous importance and creates difficulties for the schools. It is now the responsibility of the government to draw upon the information that the Swann Report contains and to implement the various strategies it details. But there must be political commitment if there is going to be a real impact.

In this paper I have not hesitated to point out the weaknesses in the Swann Report. They are there for all to see and , as a member of the Committee, it would be dishonest of me to pretend they were not there. With all its failings, however, I believe that its achievement must be that of summarizing the current situation in British schools and presenting it in a way that enables and invites action to right the wrongs suffered by ethnic minorities; and I advisedly use the word 'wrongs' since the issue is *now* not that of intellectual concern (a field of study to be pursued), it is a moral issue of right and wrong.

There were once many arguments advanced in defence of slavery. People claimed that its abolition would cause the economic collapse of the cotton growers in particular, and the southern states of America in general; that there would be worldwide consequences of incalculable magnitude; and that the slaves would suffer as a result of their freedom. In the end, slavery was abolished because the deprivation of freedom was perceived to be an evil that could not be tolerated.

The conclusions that can be drawn from the Swann Report are clear and allied with the other research findings. We know that men, women and children are suffering from economic, educational and social disadvantage because of race. It is now time for government policies to be clearly defined and machinery, including mainstream legislation, to be put in place which attacks racial discrimination not just in schools and other educational institutions – they do not exist in a vacuum – but in society at large. It is useless to create islands of equal opportunity in schools (even if that were possible). Black and Asian children live most of their lives in the wider society and when they leave school they should be able to look confidently for jobs appropriate to their abilities and aptitudes; they should be able to look for promotion by right of achievement; and to look for mutual respect with their white peers that derives from common humanity.

I take this to be the message of the Swann Report. It may create yet more fields in which we, as academics and researchers, may profitably graze. But it also lays upon us, on society at large and government in particular, a moral obligation to attack the wrongs which it reflects in the mirror it holds up to our society.

References

SWANN REPORT. GREAT BRITAIN. DEPARTMENT OF EDUCATION AND SCIENCE (1985). *Committee of Inquiry into the Education of Children from Ethnic Minority Groups. Education for All*, Cmnd 9453. London: HMSO.

VERMA, G.K. and ASHWORTH, B. (1986). *Ethnicity and Education in British Schools*. London: Macmillan.

3   'Swann's Song': the Origins, Ideology and Implications of Education for All[1]

Barry Troyna

In 1978 the then Labour government agreed to establish a Committee of Inquiry into the Education of Children from Ethnic Minority Groups. Finally in 1985 after numerous changes in personnel (including the 'resignation' of the original chairperson) the committee produced its final report. Called *Education for All* , it extended to 807 pages, had cost £692,618 to produce and was on sale at £24. Its role was to stimulate changes along multicultural lines throughout the various strata of the English education system. In short, it was intended to legitimate the educational orthodoxy of multicultural education.

In this article I argue that this goal could never be achieved. To sustain this argument, I look at the political origins of the Committee, its original and then formal terms of reference, the ideological straitjacket within which it functioned and its tenuous relationship with the core of educational decision-making in the UK. I conclude that the Committee's impact on the mitigation of racial inequalities in the education system will be minimal. Indeed, it is an issue which the Committee failed to engage with throughout its long history.

Introduction

'. . . the strangest dog's breakfast ever to emerge from HMSO . . .'

[1] This article was first published in *The Journal of Education Policy* (1986), 1, 2, 171–81 (© Taylor and Francis Ltd). It is reproduced with permission.

is how *The Times* greeted the publication of *Education for All* in its editorial of 15 March 1985. But even this inelegant epithet was mild compared to what had appeared six months earlier in the columns of the *Daily Telegraph* and, more especially, the *Daily Mail*. Based on carefully orchestrated leaks about what would be recommended in the Report, both newspapers set about creating the impression that Lord Swann and his Committee were about to suggest radical changes to the content and structure of the English education system. Changes along multicultural lines would encourage a 'white backlash' according to the *Telegraph*. Less restrained and more offensive was Mary Kenny's article for the *Daily Mail* (3 September 1984). Headlined Race Madness, Kenny castigated the Committee in her article for its presumed support for the obligatory provision in *every school* of Creole, Gujerati and Punjabi and for the adoption by 'all local authorities' of 'reverse discrimination' *(sic)* in the recruitment of black teachers. For Kenny, the apparent 'racial harmony' now existing between students in UK schools would be put 'in jeopardy' should the government accept Swann's recommendations. Her advice, then, was that 'The whole report should be scrapped, lock, stock and barrel – in the interests of the ethnic minorities as much as anyone else'. Not that criticism of the Report has been confined exclusively to right-wing ideologues such as Kenny. On the contrary, *Education for All* has also been criticized heavily by organizations such as the National Anti-racist Movement in Education, which has insisted that the Report suffers from important omissions and commissions and that it has inhibited rather than advanced the legitimation of anti-racist education (NAME, 1985). A cursory glance at what is commonly termed the 'ethnic media' in the period immediately following publication of the Report, and attention to the heated debates and critical rejoinders to *Education for All* at the various post-Swann conferences up and down the country would reveal just how much black and white anti-racists were dissatisfied with the Report. Even members of the Committee (past and present) have publicly attacked and/or dissented from some of the themes and conclusions of the Report.

Even more have dissociated themselves from Lord Swann's 'personal overview' of the full Report; 'a guided tour' to the Report which bears only tangential resemblance to its parent document but which, because of its brevity, is likely to be widely read.

Barry Hugill has suggested that dissatisfaction about *Education for All* is well-based because 'The saddest aspect of the Report is that the majority of recommendations have been made time and time again . . . At its weakest, the Report perpetuates some of the myths that it is, in another context, intent on exploding' (1985, p.13).

The pertinence and veracity of Hugill's comments can be demonstrated especially in relation to the Committee's inquiry into black 'educational underachievement' and its development of the ostensibly new, unifying concept of 'Education for All'. The first of these constitutes a linking theme of governmental concern about the education of black students; we shall see that it inspired the setting up of the Committee in the late 1970s and provided the platform on which 'Education for All' has been largely based. On the latter, neither the orthodoxy nor its constituent features, are new, in themselves. But with the growing demand for the maintenance and provision of community languages (or 'mother tongue' as it is often known) and separate schools, there was a correlative need for the state to construct an ideology to assuage the anxieties of black parents that the education system is failing to respond adequately or appropriately to the needs of their children. These issues, it seems to me, should constitute the focus of a critical review of the Report. At the same time, we must not ignore the Secretary of State's official response to the Report or the general implications of 'Education for All' in the mobilization of strategies geared towards the mitigation of racial inequalities in education.

It is important also, however, to appreciate the socio-political context in which the committee was established. After all, it is against this background that hopes and expectations of the Report were formulated. To begin with, then, I want to spend some time in delineating the political history of the Swann (formerly Rampton) Committee since its inception in the late 1970s. *En route* I want to discuss why it was established, the role it was assigned in relation to the core of educational decision-making, and the political dramas with which it has been associated. Again, this constitutes a significant part of the backcloth against which expectations were formed.

The Long Voyage: from Rampton to Swann, 1977–1985

Education for All was finally published in March 1985. At least two years late and more than eight years after the then Labour government had agreed to the request from the Select Committee on Race Relations and Immigration that it should establish 'a high level and independent inquiry into the causes of the underachievement of children of West Indian origin . . .' (1978, p.xx). It is important to reflect on the reasons why the Select Committee's concern with black 'educational underachievement' should have stimulated this positive response from central government.[1] After all, this was not a new issue of concern; in fact, since the 1960s researchers in different parts of the country (but especially in Inner London) had claimed to have identified this pattern (see Taylor, 1981; Tomlinson, 1983, pp. 26–33, for discussion). What was clear by 1978, however, was that contrary to earlier diagnoses and prognoses, black 'educational underachievement' as measured by these researchers could no longer be considered an ephemeral problem, related causally to the disruptive effects of immigration on black students, their lack of familiarity with the UK or because of discontinuities between UK and Caribbean education systems. By the late 1970s the vast majority of school students of Afro-Caribbean origin had been born and brought up in the UK; despite this, they were still more likely than their white or 'Asian' counterparts to be represented in the lower streams of the secondary school, in ESN schools and among those leaving school with few, if any, formal qualifications. For black parents and community activists, the reasons for 'underachievement' could be located within the state system of education which routinely and systematically miseducated their children. It is, therefore, no coincidence that at precisely the same time as the government agreed to investigate this phenomenon we were witnessing the mobilization of black community action in education and the accelerated growth of black supplementary or Saturday Schools. In the words of Mel Chevannes, who helped found the Black Arrow Supplementary School in Wolverhampton in 1977: 'We believe black children aren't getting the best from local schools – they need the qualifications to get the jobs – and we aim to give it to them' (quoted in Tomlinson, 1984, p.68). But while the pattern of black 'educational underachievement' and the consequent

growth of supplementary schools clearly challenged the merito-
cratic credibility of the state's education system, it would be naîve
to assume that this alone precipitated the government's response.
The typification of black youth in the educational term of
'underachievement' resonated with broader and more politically –
based characterizations of these youths as 'alienated' 'criminalized'
'disaffected' and so on (see Fisher and Joshua, 1982). Once the
'immigrant'/'stranger' hypothesis of 'underachievement' had been
stripped through the passage of time of all explanatory power, the
evidence of persistent inequalities of educational outcome and its
implications for social and political cohesion became increasingly
more obvious. As Jenny Williams and I have argued elsewhere, the
amelioration of 'underachievement' was seen as a way of forestal-
ling 'alienation' and 'rebellion' (1985, p.23). It was a relationship
not lost on the Select Committee:[2].

> The Committee consider that the relative under-achievement of
> West Indian children seriously affects their future employment
> prospects and is a matter of major importance both in educa-
> tional terms and *in the context of race relations*. (1978, p.xx;
> emphasis added)

The Select Committee's request for an inquiry to focus on the
causes of 'underachievement' among 'West Indian' students was
modified in the government's insistence that this should be based
within a more broadly conceived examination of 'the achievements
and needs of all pupils for education for life in a multi-racial
society' (ibid. p.7). At the same time, it was agreed that 'priority
should be given to identifying weaknesses in the educational
system affecting the achievement of pupils of West Indian origin'
(ibid. p.7). Now this is interesting because when the formal terms
of reference were announced by Mark Carlisle[3] in July 1979, this
emphasis on the educational system had been eschewed in favour
of an inquiry into 'the educational needs and attainments of pupils
of West Indian origin . . .' (Swann, 1985, p.vii). Inevitably this has
had profound implications for the nature of the Inquiry and for the
reception accorded both the Interim and the Final Report. After
all, criticism has crystallized largely around the Committee's
failure to consider the manifest forms of racism in schools and the
way these might impinge on the educational advancement of black

students. If the original, albeit informal, terms of reference had not been changed by Carlisle, it is likely that the Committee would have paid considerably more attention to precisely those in-school processes which black and white anti-racists have argued have been ignored. What is more, as we shall see, it would have been more difficult for Carlisle and Sir Keith Joseph to reject claims that racism in education constitutes an important phenomenon for investigation and action.

On publication of the Committee's Interim Report, *West Indian Children in our Schools,* in 1981, John Rex was prompted to write that: 'The most important thing about the Rampton Committee, as it used to be called, is not its content, but the whole political drama which surrounded the publication of its first report' (1981, p.4). It is difficult to dissent from this view. To begin with, there was an inexplicable delay of four months between submission to the DES and publication. In the Parliamentary debate on the Report, in July 1981, Tom Ellis asked whether 'the report would have been published if there had been no Brixton . . . disturbances in the intervening period'. Ellis's criticism was based on the view that, first, the DES had provided inspired leaks to the press in this period which had served to discredit the Report in advance, and secondly, that the DES had failed to respond formally to the 20 recommendations aimed specifically at it. Controversy also surrounded the 'resignation' of the chairperson, Anthony Rampton, in May 1981; did he jump or was he pushed is a question which continues to tantalize. Certainly, there were suggestions that Carlisle was unhappy about the emphasis placed in the Report on racism as an explanation of black 'educational underachievement'. Nevertheless, it is salutary to recall that 'racism' constituted only one of the possible contributors to 'underachievement' and that the others crystallized around a range of pathologies including poor family background, lack of parental support and understanding, inadequate socialization, and so on. Rex's comment also draws our attention to the fact that the Report suffered from a paucity of credible research evidence and an inadequate interpretation of that which was at hand. The Committee based its general argument about black 'educational underachievement' on data provided by the DES School Leavers Survey 1978–79. This purported to show – and the Committee concurred with the impression – that in the six LEAs considered students of

Afro-Caribbean origin performed significantly less well in public examinations than either white indigenous students or those of south Asian origin. The failure of the Committee to standardize these data along social class lines or to consider the results in relation to gender differences and individual schools' records of achievement has been highlighted and discussed elsewhere (Reeves and Chevannes, 1981; Troyna, 1984a). The point I want to make here is that the grossly insensitive use of the data, linked as it was to the provocative issue of teacher racism, undermined the credibility of the committee's argument, failed to pre-empt inevitable press criticism of the Report and incurred the anger of many teachers who perceived it as an (unjustified) attack on their professionalism.[4] We shall see later that, like the Bourbons, the Committee chaired by Lord Swann since Rampton's 'resignation', had 'learned nothing and forgotten nothing' in its handling of comparable data in the final Report.

The DES response to the Interim Report – or more precisely its non-response – might also be seen as more significant than the content of the document. On its publication, Carlisle had insisted in response to a written question that he would 'consult widely on the Report's implications' (HC, 17 June 1981, col. 240) and this was reaffirmed by Rhodes Boyson in the Parliamentary debate, less than three weeks later. But neither this nor a formal response from the DES to Rampton's recommendations took place. DES action was confined to circulating the report to LEAs, without comment, and organizing a one-day conference! What we have, then, is a Committee charged with making 'definite and positive recommendations' but which has remained structurally peripheral to national policy-making and developments in education (Dorn and Troyna, 1982). Again, this was confirmed by Sir Keith Joseph's perfunctory acknowledgement of the Swann committee's contribution (Troyna and Ball, forthcoming).

To sum up this section: these brief glimpses into the origins, activities and recommendations of the Rampton Committee and the official responses it generated help us to contextualize more appropriately the Swann Report, its emphases and ideological framework. It allows us to do this for a number of reasons. First, we have seen that, at least after the Conservative Party secured power in 1979, the Inquiry was never intended to focus on the school as an agent for the reproduction of racial inequalities. If anything, its official terms of reference geared it towards explicating cultural and social phenomena which might be associated with differential performance between students from different ethnic backgrounds. The legacy of Carlisle's reformulation of the Committee's original terms of reference can be found not only in the final Report, but also in the nature of the research it attempted, but failed, to commission. Secondly, its relationship to formal decision-making structures in education was, from its inception, minimal and subordinate. That is to say, as a consultative committee, first and foremost, it was expected to present recommendations for action; but the Secretary of State was not compelled to accept them. Thirdly, and most significantly, its concern with · black 'educational underachievement' was inextricably linked to the broader political rather than specifically educational implications of a discernible group of students getting a raw deal from their schooling. In this sense, Rampton/Swann shared many of the concerns and imperatives associated with earlier government inquiries chaired by Hunt, Newsom and Plowden, among others. The goal was to identify reformist policies which might secure an integrated society; in other words, stabilize a society characterized by social, political and 'racial' divisions. The ideology of 'Education for All' and the recommendations it prompted need to be seen in this broader historical and socio-political context, one which is essentially reactive in its concern and pre-emptive in its goal: as the Swann Committee put it in their final Report:

> We believe that unless major efforts are made to reconcile the concerns and aspirations of both the majority and minority communities along more genuinely pluralist lines, there is a real risk of the fragmentation of our society along ethnic lines which would seriously threaten the stability and cohesion of society as a whole. (1985, p.7)

'Underachievement' Revisited

By the time Lord Swann and his colleagues submitted their final Report to the DES, apprehensions of and reformist challenges to racial inequalities in education had shifted quite perceptibly. No longer is the multicultural education debate focused exclusively on the formulation of responses to what white educationists define as the 'special needs' of black students. Instead, the last few years have seen growing support, at a formal and informal level in LEAs and individual schools, for 'racialized' conceptions of educational change. That is to say, there is a growing demand for changes in policy and practice which implicate all staff and students, irrespective of the ethnic composition of the area or school (see Troyna and Williams, 1985). At the same time, concern about the apparently immutable pattern of 'West Indian underachievement' has persisted. In the period following publication of Rampton's Interim Report both the Home Affairs Committee and Lord Scarman drew attention to this trend and to the disturbing political and social implications it apparently gives rise to. In the words of the Home Affairs Committee it is evident that 'we have not got ethnic minority education right' (1981), p.1.v). For Swann the imperative was clear: to delineate the extent of black 'educational underachievement', to specify its causes and to formulate an ideology which in practice would ameliorate this educational and social evil.

But it seems to me that this is a restricted and restrictive research paradigm. It is *restricted* because it demands attention to achievement levels along ethnic lines. Consequently, the Committee's discussion and conclusions were based solely on a comparative investigation of the performance of 'Asian', 'West Indian' and 'All other leavers' (i.e. mainly whites) in public examinations taken in five LEAs in 1981–82. Apart from the occasional genuflection towards the importance of class and gender as explanatory, or at least moderating, variables, the focus was on explicating differences or otherwise between the achievement levels of students from these different ethnic backgrounds; nothing more or less. By replicating the Rampton Committee's mode of analysis, Swann and his colleagues showed a cynical disregard for the criticisms of this approach already voiced by Reeves and Chevannes (1981), Rex (1981) and Troyna (1984a), among others. Also ignored was the important research published in 1983 by Ken Roberts and his associates which had shown that the national profile of black 'educational underachievement' could be 'attributable entirely to the fact that they reside in districts and attend schools where the attainments of all pupils are below average' (1983, p.19). One final point needs to be made here. The Committee's determination to look for differences between ethnic groups not only blinded it to the influences of gender, class and individual school performance records, it also led them to ignore the significance of age. As my colleague Krutika Tanna has shown (1985), a critical reading of the data provided by the DES has revealed that 'Asians' tend to perform as well as 'All other leavers' only after investing more of their time in formal education. In other words, in order for them to achieve comparable results with 'All other leavers' they need to stay on at school longer and give up the opportunities provided by apprenticeship courses and YTS, both of which have an upper age limit which prevents entry.

The Swann Committee also operated within a *restrictive* paradigm. This is because having concluded on the basis of the data that 'West Indians' perform less well and 'Asians' performed at least on a par with 'All other leavers', the Committee was compelled to identify and attribute causal status to characteristics which were peculiar to particular ethnic groups. This had a number of unfortunate consequences, to say the least. First, it provided the space for critics to challenge the proposition that racism has an inhibiting effect on the educational progress of black students. As Simon Pearce wrote in his policy paper for the Monday Club: 'Most Asians perform as well as whites, and considerably better than West Indians. What then of racism?' (1985, p.3; see also Jeffcoate, 1984, p.64; NAS/UWT, n.d., for similar critiques). Secondly, it steered the Committee into commissioning an extensive review of literature and research on 'The IQ Question' simply to re-affirm that it is '*not* a significant factor in underachievement' (1985, p.89; emphasis in original). One might have hoped that the Committee would already have been sufficiently aware of the pseudo-scientific and racist predicates of intelligence testing through the writings of Flynn (1980), Kamin(1977) and Rose (1979). Finally, it led to the reproduction and quasi-legitimation of cultural stereotypes in a forlorn attempt to explain the different achievement levels of 'West Indians' and 'Asians'. The former, we are told, 'are given to "protest" and "a high profile" '; the latter are more concerned with '"keeping their heads down" and adopting "a low profile"' (1985, p.86). Not only are these stereotypes offensive and racist, they are indisputably wrong.[5] But even if we suspend our judgement on this matter and tolerate Swann's conclusion that 'the reasons for the very different school performances of Asians and West Indians seem likely to lie deep within their respective cultures' (ibid., p.87), how then is it possible to acccount for the educational performance of Bangladeshi students – 'the one Asian sub-group whose school achievement was very low indeed', according to the Committee (loc. cit.)?

The point I want to stress here is quite simple: the Swann Committee, unable to escape from the confines of its original problematic, generated and reproduced a number of untenable propositions and ended up in a cul-de-sac. Its failure to win the consent of the black communities for a piece of original research into the question of 'underachievement' can be explained largely in terms of its insistence that ethnic cultures as well as in-school processes needed to be examined. But do they? Surely the findings from the Thomas Coram Institute which show that standards of literacy and numeracy among black children are as high as those of whites when they first go to school (*TES*, 23 December 1983), coupled with Michael Rutter's conclusion that black students are prepared to invest extra years in their schooling after which they leave with a 'broadly comparable' set of qualifications to whites (Rutter *et al.*, 1982, p.163), suggests that the problems which black students experience occur during the '15,000 hours' of their school career. From this perspective it is difficult to dispute NAME's insistence that Swann should have commissioned research to consider 'some of the major factors which impinge on success or failure in schools'; namely, 'Institutional racism, gateways, barriers, "filter systems", streaming, setting, suspensions, expulsions, referral procedures, assessment centres, "Sin bins", remedial units, mixed ability teaching, guidance and option choices, timetabling, levels of parental and community involvement, and consultation and pastoral care' (1985, p.2). Only research could identify how far each of these embrace racist impulses, intent, practices or consequences.

Swann's Song of 'Education for All'

But Swann's conception of racism is based on an entirely different predicate, one which believes that it is derived largely from ignorance; thus it is seen neither as a uniquely British phenomenon or a problem peculiar to 'whites' (1985, p.27).

Instead it is said to constitute little more than ignorance and misunderstanding about the life-styles and cultural values of ethnic minority communities. The imperative for the education system, then, is 'to equip a pupil with knowledge and understanding in place of ignorance and to develop his or her ability to formulate views and attitudes and to assess and judge situations on the basis of this knowledge' (ibid., p.14). Racism, in other words, is synonymous with prejudice in this ideological framework[6] and the task becomes one of persuading different sections of the education system, and the state in general, of the educational efficacy of the orthodoxy, 'Education for All' (ibid., pp.87-8). But in order to ensure the success of this strategy the black communities, according to the Committee, must play their part. Thus, despite considerable support for separate schools, especially from South Asian communities, the Committee declined to support these initiatives; the reason: the ' "separate development" of all different groups would be unlikely to offer equality or justice to the members of all groups, least of all the numerically smaller minorities' (ibid., p.5). From this same vantage-point of a commitment to 'a democratic pluralist society' the Committee expressed reservations about 'mother tongue' teaching in schools. It neither supported 'the introduction of programmes of bilingual education in this country' or the maintenance of 'mother tongue' in mainstream schools (ibid., p.406). Rather the Committee maintained that:[7]

> . . . the key to equality of opportunity, to academic success and, more broadly, to participation on equal terms as a full member of society, is good command of *English* and the emphasis must therefore we feel be on the learning of English. (ibid., p.407; emphasis in original)

Without wishing to deny the importance of fluency in English, it is important to point out – as earlier sections of the Report indicated – that this ability has *not* helped students of Afro-Caribbean origin to secure 'equality of opportunity' in UK society (see Brown, 1984; Troyna, 1984b, for discussion.) Nor can the denial of community language provision be sustained legitimately in the context of arguments for 'a democratic pluralist society'. As J.J. Smolicz has argued, language constitutes a core value for certain ethnic minority communities and, contrary to Swann's implicit assumption that the focus on learning English will facilitate the emergence of a stable and cohesive society, evidence drawn from the Canadian experience indicates that: 'Conflict and division arise not out of difference, but rather out of denial of the right and the opportunity to be different' (Smolicz, 1981, p.137). Swann's rejection of community demands for the legitimation of 'mother tongue' provision and teaching in schools and for separate schooling for the purpose of maintaining the 'core values' of certain ethnic minority groups, therefore, seems likely to engender precisely those feelings of discontent, lack of identification with the state, frustration and demands for structural separatism which 'Education for All' is intent on preventing.

And what does Swann offer in return for these community concessions? A conception of the state which is neutral, which will be responsive to the call for anti-racism and which is waiting to be provided with the technical means by which it may operationalize this orthodoxy. As the Committee asserts: 'countering racism within society must be a matter for the Law, for Government, Local Authorities, Employers, the Commission for Racial Equality and indeed many others, individually and collectively' (1985, pp.87–8). This complacent, even cynical conception of the state's relationship with the black communities and its receptivity to calls for anti-racism has been highlighted elsewhere (Troyna and Williams, 1985; Hatcher and Shallice, 1983). Suffice it to say here that in presenting the Report to Parliament, the Secretary of State carefully diminished the importance of racism in education, a point not lost on Giles Radice MP. He asked Joseph *why* he had ignored racism, a factor 'which blights the prospects of many black and Asian children'. Joseph's reply should come as little surprise, except perhaps to the Swann Committee:[8]

> The hon. Gentleman has allowed himself to speak in far too absolute a fashion about what he calls 'racism'. He does an injustice to the teaching force, whose members are dedicated to the service of individual children and in whom I have seen precious little evidence of any racist prejudice. (HC, 14 March 1985, col. 437)

The truth or falsity of Joseph's assertion is a matter for empirical inquiry although, parenthetically, it is worth noting that Peter Green (1982) found that some teachers are prejudiced in their engagement with black students, while Peter Figueroa (1983) has found that many teachers operate with a 'racial frame of reference' which also disadvantages black students. The point I want to stress here, however, is that individual teacher prejudice is only part of the story of racism in the English educational system. Both Joseph and the Swann Committee fail, or refuse, to consider the more insidious and covert forms of racism as they operate almost routinely in pedagogic, administrative and organizational features of school and college life.

In all, the arguments provided in *Education for All* circumvent the central problem of how to provide anti-racist education in multiracist Britain. And it was avoided by two principal methods. First, through defining racism in terms of prejudice and recommending teaching strategies to combat those attitudes (among students), and racism awareness training (RAT) courses to eradicate them (supposedly) from the teaching profession. Secondly, through the proposition that the state is willing to accept clearly formulated arguments for initiating and endorsing anti-racism as an educational and political orthodoxy. Both are contentious, if not erroneous propositions. But in the course of this political chicanery the Committee succeeded in denying the legitimacy of certain demands from the UK's black communities, obfuscated the thrust of the debate by failing to consider and identify how racism operates in the education system, and eschewed responsibility for reformulating the education system, so that it might cater more effectively and appropriately for its ethnically diverse clientele. What we are left with, then, is a Report which advocates certain superficial changes to the structure, orientation and content of the contemporary education system and further endorsement for those multiculturalists committed to the development of a pluralist society through the promotion and acknowledgement of ethnic life-styles in the classroom. Put another way, Swann and his colleagues have provided little support or encouragement for those interested in and committed to the racialization of educational policy and practice; for those, in other words, who are committed to 'minimizing racial inequalities and discrimination by first identifying where these are present' (Troyna and Williams, 1985, p.5). For educationists and bureaucrats, on the other hand, committed to 'cultural tourism' or the three Ss (Saris, Samosas and Steel Bands) conception of educational change, 'Swann's song' will constitute an important weapon in their ideological armoury.

Notes

I am grateful to Wendy Ball and Bob Burgess for their perceptive comments on an earlier draft of this article.

[1] My reservations about the conceptual precision and methodological basis of the term black 'educational underachievement' have been outlined elsewhere (Troyna, 1984a).

[2] This was not the first time that a governmental body had drawn attention to the relationship between poor school performance and political and social unrest (see Solomos, 1983; Troyna, 1984b).

[3] Although Shirley Williams, as Secretary of State in the Labour government, had agreed to the establishment of the Committee and had appointed Anthony Rampton to the chair, her successor in the newly elected Conservative government appointed the committee's members and specified its formal terms of reference.

[4] The publication of the Report coincided more or less with the School's Council decision to publish a heavily censored version of its commissioned study into multicultural education. It was censored precisely because it purported to show in the original version the prevalence of teacher racism, a finding which angered the teacher unions.

[5] Consider, for instance, whether a 'low profile' was adopted by Asians at the Imperial Typewriters dispute, Grunwick, Bradford, Newham, and so on. See selected chapters in CCCS (1982) for discussion of the form of commonsense racism articulated by Swann and others.

[6] This is especially true of Lord Swann's personal 'guided tour' to the Report. There the term, racism, is omitted entirely in favour of the concepts, 'prejudice' and 'discrimination' (Swann, 1985, p.2). Implicit in this ideological scenario is the claim that black citizens and their children experience only individualized forms of racialism, whereas the evidence elsewhere indicates the pervasiveness and institutionalized nature of racism in contemporary UK society (see, for example, Cashmore and Troyna, 1983).

[7] This overwhelming emphasis on competence in English as the key to equality of opportunity in the UK once again highlights the linkage between *Education for All* and previous governmental inquiries in this sphere (Troyna and Williams, 1985, chapter 1).

[8] Wendy Ball and I have considered the government's response to Swann in more detail elsewhere (Troyna and Ball, forthcoming).

References

BROWN, C. (1984). *Black and White Britain: the Third PSI Survey.* London: Heinemann.

CASHMORE, E. and TROYNA, B. (1983). *Introduction to Race Relations.* London: Routledge and Kegan Paul.

CENTRE FOR CONTEMPORARY CULTURAL STUDIES (1982). *The Empire Strikes Back.* London: Hutchinson.

DORN, A. and TROYNA, B. (1982). 'Multiracial education and the politics of decision-making', *Oxford Review of Education*, 8, 2, 175–185.

FIGUEROA, P. (1983). 'Race relations and cultural differences: some ideas on a racial frame of reference'. In: VERMA, G.K., and BAGLEY, C. (Eds) *Race Relations and Cultural Differences.* Beckenham: Croom Helm, pp.15–28.

FISHER, G. and JOSHUA, H. (1982). 'Social policy and black youth'. In: CASHMORE, E. and TROYNA, B. (Eds) *Black Youth in Crisis.* London: Allen and Unwin, pp.129–142.

FLYNN. J.R. (1980). *Race, IQ and Jensen.* London: Routledge and Kegan Paul.

GREEN, P. (1982). 'Tolerance, teaching and the self-concept in the multi-ethnic classroom', *Multi-Ethnic Education*, 1, pp.8–11.

HATCHER, R. and SHALLICE, J. (1983). 'The politics of anti-racist education', *Multiracial Education*, 12, 1, pp.3–21.

HOME OFFICE (1978). *The West Indian Community: Observations on the Report of the Select Committee on Race Relations and Immigration*, Cmnd 7186. London: HMSO.

HOUSE OF COMMONS (1981). *Fifth Report from the Home Affairs Committee Session 1980–1981: Racial Disadvantage*, Vol. 1. London: HMSO.

HUGILL, B. (1985). 'Five years' frustration', *New Statesman*, 18 January, pp.12–13.

JEFFCOATE, R. (1984). *Ethnic Minorities and Education*. London: Harper and Row.

KAMIN, L.J. (1977). *The Science and Politics of IQ*. Harmondsworth: Penguin.

NAS/UWT (n.d.) *Multi-Ethnic Education*. London: NAS/UWT.

NATIONAL ANTIRACIST MOVEMENT IN EDUCATION (1985). *NAME on Swann*, Nottingham: NAME.

PEARCE, S. (1985). *Education and the Multi-Racial Society*. London: The Monday Club.

RAMPTON REPORT. GREAT BRITAIN. DEPARTMENT OF EDUCATION AND SCIENCE (1981). *West Indian Children in our Schools*, Cmnd 8723. London: HMSO.

REEVES, F. and CHEVANNES, M. (1981), 'The underachievement of Rampton', *Multiracial Education*, 12, 1, pp.35–42.

REX , J. (1981). 'Culture clashes', *Times Educational Supplement*, 7 August, p.4.

ROBERTS, K. *et al.* (1983). 'Young, black and out of work'. In: TROYNA, B. and SMITH, D.I. (Eds) *Racism, School and the Labour Market*. Leicester: National Youth Bureau.

ROSE, S. (1979). 'Race, intelligence and education', *New Community*, 7, 2, pp.280–283.

RUTTER, M. *et al.* (1982). *School Experiences and Achievements and the First Year of Employment*. Unpublished report to the DES.

SELECT COMMITTEE ON RACE RELATIONS AND IMMIGRATION (1978). *The West Indian Community*, Vol 1. London: HMSO.

SMOLICZ, J.J. (1981). 'Cultural pluralism and educational policy: in search of stable multiculturalism', *Australian Journal of Education*, 25, 2, pp.121–145

SOLOMOS, J. (1983). *The Politics of Black Youth Unemployment*. Working Papers on Ethnic Relations No. 20. Birmingham: Research Unit on Ethnic Relations, Aston University.

SWANN, M. (1985). *Education for All: A Brief Guide to the Main Issues of the Report*. London:HMSO.

SWANN REPORT. GREAT BRITAIN. DEPARTMENT OF EDUCATION AND SCIENCE (1985). *Committee of Inquiry into the Education of Children from Ethnic Minority Groups. Education for All*, Cmnd 9453. London. HMSO.

TANNA, K. (1985). 'Opening the black box', *Times Educational Supplement*, 20 September, p.27.

TAYLOR, M. (1981). *Caught Between. A Review of Research into the Education of Pupils of West Indian Origin.* Windsor: NFER-NELSON

TOMLINSON, S. (1983). *Ethnic Minorities in British Schools.* London: Heinemann.

TOMLINSON, S. (1984). *Home and School in Multicultural Britain.* London: Batsford.

TROYNA, B. (1984a). 'Fact or artefact? The "Educational underachievement" of black pupils', *British Journal of Sociology of Education*, 5, 2, pp.153–166.

TROYNA, B. (1984b). 'Multicultural education: emancipation or containment?' In: BARTON, L. and WALKER, S. (Eds) *Social Crisis and Educational Research.* Beckenham: Croom Helm, pp.75–97.

TROYNA, B. and BALL, W. (forthcoming). 'Partnerships, consultation and influence: state rhetoric in the struggle for racial equality'. In: HARTNETT, A. and NAISH, M. (Eds) *Education and Society Today.* Lewes: Falmer Press.

TROYNA, B. and WILLIAMS, J. (1985), *Racism, Education and the State: the Racialisation of Education Policy,* Beckenham: Croom Helm.

4   The Swann Report: an LEA Response

Winifred Mould

Three post-Swann conferences were held in Tyne and Wear during 1986. The first, organized jointly by the Newcastle University Faculty of Education and the Tyne and Wear Community Relations Council, was held in early January. The second, organized by the Newcastle branch of the National Anti-racist Movement in Education, was held in late January and the third is the British Sociological Association's conference, held in Sunderland. Some 250 participants listened and discussed. However, the real message from Swann was for positive action to follow constructive discourse.

My standpoint is as a practitioner not from a philosophical, theoretical or altruistic stance, but as someone who is required to translate the Swann recommendations into action in a local education authority. It must not be supposed that LEAs' philosophies and practices with regard to multicultural education are consistent with government thinking. In some instances their practices will precede government recommendations, in others they will lag behind.

These differences in commitment to the philosophy of multicultural education are as a result of the great independence and power of local authorities to determine their own policies. This decentralized educational system means that important decisions concerning curriculum development are taken at local level, very often by the teachers themselves. Central government can stimulate developments, but appears reluctant to impose any control by legislation. It would appear, however, that a firmer directional control by government is being gained, through the allocation of such funding as Educational Support Grants, which encourage LEAs to promote curriculum changes in areas identified centrally. However in this enterprise, the development of multicultural education, involving many interests, it is clear that local authorities play a major role in determining policy.

I should like to approach the issue of applying the principles identified in the Swann Report from the point of view of my own experiences in this field in two education authorities in Tyne and Wear, those of North and South Tyneside.

What effect can a document such as the Swann Report have on an area which is predominantly working class, and where there are few visible signs of identifiable minority groups? In the harsh economic climate of the north-east what hope is there of a good 'education for all'? Let it not be thought at the outset that no action had taken place with regard to multicultural education in these authorities prior to Swann. From approximately 1977, at the beginning of the Rampton deliberations, there was a growing awareness that some special educational programmes were required to meet the needs of the relatively few ethnic minority children in the area. I doubt whether at this time it was realized that there was also a need for either curriculum development, or curriculum modification, for all children to reflect the multi-ethnic nature of British society. The reason for such lack of awareness was because multicultural education was considered to be compensatory education for black, underachieving pupils, and since there were very few such children in the area, multicultural education was not regarded as necessary. In the early 1980s the most common phrases used by headteachers when discussing the relevance of multicultural education to their schools were:

We have no problems here.
We treat all children in the same way.
My catchment area is not multicultural.

These local reactions, in the 1980s, to the concept of multicultural education reflected those shown in the 1960s by areas which had experienced earlier immigration. It seems likely that the Tyneside authorities felt little urgency in recognizing the needs and contributions of minority groups until their presence in the area was clearly evidenced.

Although the 1981 Census had shown that New Commonwealth citizens constituted some 4 per cent of the overall population in the UK, in Tyne and Wear this percentage was only 0.82 per cent. The largest single minority group in the area was the Irish with a 0.38 per cent representation. Both the North and South Tyneside authorities had experienced previous immigration from discharged seamen, and Indians, Arabs, Somalis, Malayans and Africans had established homes in the area.

Apart from what were described as the 'race riots' of 1919 and 1930, when it was suggested that white and black seamen fought for the few available berths on ships, relationships between majority and minority groups did not appear to present difficulties. However, these past experiences of immigrant settlement conditioned many teachers to expect that the minority groups would adapt to the white, British way of life, and that there was no necessity to provide either compensatory education for blacks or for the curriculum in the schools to reflect the diversity of British society.

What the two authorities did provide initially was support for English as a second language, most often on a withdrawal base, and for some secondary pupils, in a special language unit. Any other needs ethnic minority children experienced relating to food, dress or religious days of observance were often interpreted as 'difficulties'.

From the early 1980s other events affected what was happening in schools in Tyneside. Two Department of Education and Science regional courses were held in the area. One, at Durham University in 1982, was entitled 'Towards a Curriculum for a Multicultural Society', the other held in South Tyneside in 1983 was 'Professional Responses in a Multicultural Society'. Such initiatives promoted action within schools, such as one school spending one term's work around the theme of 'The Chinese New Year'. Another school, with a small number of Muslim pupils, arranged for the imam from the local mosque to provide an alternative morning service for these children. An authority booklet *Welcome to School* was produced, in translation, for minority parents who did not speak English. Perhaps such initiatives belonged to Chris Mullard's 'integrationist' phase of multicultural education, with a preoccupation with 'difference' and with 'quaintness' (1982). Critics of such initiatives will say that it still embodied the racial structure of power that dominated and reproduced a class system in which blacks had no say, and where blacks were still regarded as disadvantaged and underachieving and, unfortunately, as 'problems'.

We are all aware that there are influences outside the school buildings which affect policy within an education authority; the political ideology of the elected members; the ability of pressure groups to promote or hinder initiatives; the current economic climate; the often conflicting demands of other worthy causes; and the support and direction given by the DES, these are important determinants of change. Similarly, there are forces within the school which work both towards and against change: teacher attitudes; pupil attitudes; allocation of available resources; insufficient resources; insufficient staff expertise; teacher union industrial action; low status of proposed action; self-help teacher groups; and lack of evidenced support from senior management, again these are unquestionably important elements in the ability of an LEA to promote multicultural education.

In Tyne and Wear one pressure group, the Tyne and Wear Community Relations Council, has undeniably produced the most significant changes in the development of multicultural education within the two Tyneside authorities. It may also be credited with the relative speed with which the authorities' statements on multicultural education were produced. Established by the Race Relations Act 1968, the role of the parent body, the Commission for Racial Equality, was to promote harmonious community relations. Suspected by both blacks and whites of not representing either's needs, the Tyne and Wear CRC has steadfastly refused to support what it sees as extremist views. Perhaps because of this, perhaps in spite of this, the Tyne and Wear CRC has experienced a measure of success which appears to be denied to many other local CRCs. It has consistently lobbied elected members, education officers, minority representatives, the police and the unions to create an awareness of the needs, expectations and rights of minority groups. Regarded as anachronistic by some who pursue an anti-racist policy, and as a militant organization by others who see no reason for change, it continues to bring gentle but persistent pressure upon the five LEAs which constitute Tyne and Wear, and on whose grant aid it depends.

At regular two-monthly meetings representatives from the five local multicultural education working panels meet together and report on the progress made within their authority over the previous two months. The knowledge that other local authorities are planning and implementing changes produces a 'knock-on' effect.

In March 1983 the Tyne and Wear CRC organized a weekend conference, 'Education for Racial Harmony', to which they invited five representatives from the five LEAs – the director, chairperson of the education committee, headteachers and an adviser – as well as representatives from the minority groups within the area. The main objective of this conference was to persuade LEAs to produce their own policy statement on multicultural education. Within 16 months all five authorities had had their statements passed through council. The Tyne and Wear CRC would appear to have had a 100 per cent success rate. Whether these policy statements were merely discussion documents or statements of principle will be discussed later. Indeed, perhaps Husband's view of the limited success of local CRCs can be supported; he suggests:

> The greatest achievement of the local community relations councils has probably been to educate some of the local social and political élite, both from the majority and the minorities. With rare exception, their impact on local public opinion or on the real disadvantages of ethnic minorities appears to have been trivial, and even their successes may well, like the Urban Programme, have provided the alibi for the absence of any serious effort at local level to change local government policies and practices. (Husband, 1982).

Perhaps the Tyne and Wear CRC may prove to be the exception.

Whatever the criticisms levelled at the multicultural policy statements produced by LEAs, I think we can agree with Richardson's statement that 'a policy statement is a petard by which an LEA consciously and publicly seeks to be hoisted; a deliberate, calculated hostage to fortune, a stick for its own back to be beaten' (1983). We might also agree with Dorn and Troyna's view that in too many instances their exact relationship to the decision-making process, to the allocation of resources and to the provision of education at classroom level is unclear (1981).

However, the very method of arrival at such a policy statement can, in itself, create an awareness of the issue. In one Tyneside area the local Community Relations Council Education Working Party produced a draft policy statement. This was presented to the Director of Education who, in turn, circulated it to all headteachers, requesting them to discuss the proposals and to comment upon them by a certain date. The subsequent replies make fascinating reading and endorse the need for prejudice reduction strategies and attitude-changing techniques, discussed earlier.

Twenty per cent of schools submitted nil returns. It seems reasonable to assume that they were either indifferent to the proposals or believed they did not concern them or did not consider the issues sufficiently important to discuss. Of those schools which did reply, approximately 40 per cent of replies indicated considerable support, 40 per cent expressed certain reservations and 20 per cent were antagonistic to the proposals.

Of those who were overtly antagonistic, I should like to quote the following extracts:

> I am not prepared to be seen to be indoctrinating sub-cultures into the cultural attitudes and beliefs of the children in the school.

> We know that in certain areas throughout the country, and certainly in ——, special provision for multicultural education is not at all necessary. Our reactions were of indignation at the wording of several of the suggested policies. Certainly, no burden on time or money should be placed on normal requisition income.

> Our experience is that these children can be integrated easily and happily where they are few and far between.

> I do not believe that the UK is a multicultural, multi-racial and multi-religious society. I do, however, feel that within the UK there are minority groups who deserve to be helped to assume the white British way of life.

> Of all the issues which affect schools, in terms of our school environment, the racial/nationality/religious problem is, in our experience, no problem at all. We cannot remember one incident which had racial overtones to any significant degree.

Some schools drafted much more positive replies:

> The implementation of this policy will be a means of fostering a multicultural education in which the possibility exists for *all* groups to develop in an intellectual, confident, self-respecting fashion: people working together in an interactive, collaborative way and therefore paving the way towards anti-racism.

> Such a policy is necessary not only for its implications for national unity, but for its long-term value towards the development of international understanding.

> We feel that such a policy at this time is both necessary and relevant to the formation of a harmonious and equal society within —— and the country as a whole.

> For my part I would like —— Tyneside at least to be in a position to give a resounding 'No' to any little Hitlers that pop up.

It is evident that these replies from teachers showed the wide discrepancy of views held within the teaching profession. The local education authority must seek to find ways to change the negatively entrenched views.

It is not only the opinion and beliefs of some members of the teaching profession that we must attempt to change, it is also the views of some of the children in our schools. Although the media may have more effect on attitude formation than the schools, we must not forget that the school is still a significant agent of change.

In November, 1984 one authority arranged a series of in-service days on multicultural education for all headteachers and deputy headteachers in the borough. There was a 99 per cent turn-out of headteachers and a 72 per cent representation of deputy headteachers. In group discussion it became evident that many senior staff believed that there was no racial prejudice in their schools, no incidents of racial abuse and no feeling of white superiority. To clarify this situation, children in a number of schools were asked to produce some 'cold' writing on the topic of 'black people'. The children's work was anonymously written. Teachers were asked not to discuss the topic with the children. Scripts were received from 200 children: nine-year-olds, 13-year-olds and sixth-formers.

Headteachers warned that to ask children to participate in such an exercise was dangerous; that it would create difference and difficulties where none existed; and that instead of improving race relations, it could effectively damage them. It was found that approximately 75 per cent of these children held negative attitudes about black people and, of those, about one-third held strongly hostile attitudes. Almost all children talked of Britain as a white society, and almost all those who advocated acceptance and access to equality of opportunity did so from a paternalistic point of view, shown by the following examples:

> I think there is nothing wrong with coloured people. The problem comes when they try to take over.

> I do not like the Pakistanis. Most of them come over here to steal jobs from the English people. They think that we owe them this right, because we used to rule their country.

A number of children blamed black people for the high unemployment figures:

> They have come over and started taking our jobs and made the British unemployed. I think anyone who even looks black should be deported or they should all be sent to live in one small part of Britain, maybe Belfast.

> Soon we'll have all Africa over here ruling us. Soon we might have coloured people in the government, policemen, judges, solicitors, lawyers and barristers. White people live in this country, should rule this country and be in this country.

A great number of children mentioned the National Front, although no child identified himself or herself with this organization. They were certainly aware of some of the National Front propaganda such as: 'There ain't no black in the Union Jack.' It was refreshing to hear the views of this 13-year-old:

> I've always thought how completely stupid and infantile it is to discriminate or even single-out people due to their colour... to sneer and be horrible to people of a certain colour to me seems to hint at total mental defectiveness.

With evidence of some of the previous examples of racist attitudes, my task is made easier since I can now demonstrate to teachers the racist attitudes exhibited by some of their pupils.

What, then, does my authority need to do to implement the Swann recommendations? We have produced an implementation policy to support the multicultural education policy statement. This will be personally addressed and sent to all staff in schools, both teaching and non-teaching, to all governors of schools and to other support services. This implementation policy requires all schools and colleges to produce their own school policy statements following the authority's guidelines, and after extensive consultation between staff within the school. The school policy statement is to be submitted to school governors before being forwarded to the Director of Education. There will be an annual monitoring of progress made. As part of the implementation policy, schools are asked to devise strategies for dealing with incidents of racial abuse. These are identified as including: verbal abuse, racist graffiti, racist remarks and physical abuse. Records of such instances are to be kept and the Director of Education is to be informed. [The policy statement appears in Appendix I together with Winifred Mould's queries regarding LEA implementation.]

What do we hope to achieve by pursuing this policy? We would expect that teachers would, through self-appraisal, examine the content of their lessons and the literature which is being used, to ensure that the subject-matter is being presented fairly and accurately; that negative stereotypes of other groups are not being reproduced; and that value is given to the achievements and contributions of other nations to world development. We would expect teachers to begin to recognize that multicultural education is about this re-appraisal of what we teach, how we present our information, how we develop positive attitudes towards others and how we deal with discriminatory practices, racism and lack of educational opportunity.

When a school is formulating its own whole-school policy, we would suggest it considers the following questions:

1. Does the curriculum reflect a single viewpoint – a white, Anglo-Saxon viewpoint?
2. Are the contributions of other cultures and nations to world development recognized and valued?

3. Is the global interdependence of the world explained both historically and currently?

4. Are the children aware of the rich diversity of ethnic groups resident in the UK and the historical reasons of settlement?

5. Are these ethnic groups treated as quaint, different or objects of scorn? Are they considered as problems and blamed for their oppression?

6. What steps are taken within the school to give accurate and unbiased views of these ethnic groups reflecting their situation as it is in the present rather than as it was in the past?

7. Is the history of slavery discussed?

8. Are pupils and staff made critically aware of their own perceptions and attitudes with regard to race, culture and language?

9. Are the materials, texts and displays used in school positively selected as being free from racism, stereotyping, distortions and patronizing attitudes? If the materials being used do not positively reject these concepts, are these negative connotations identified to the children for discussion purposes?

10. Do both the overt and covert curricula emphasize the principle that all citizens within a pluralist society have equal rights and privileges?

If schools are responding positively to these ten questions, they will be implementing the Swann recommendations. However, their task is not easy and they will require considerable support. What kind of support can an authority give? Apart from the multicultural policy statement and implementation policy, in-service education must play a major role. How does an authority meet such training requirements with limited specialist staff at its disposal? With great difficulty! There are signs that the DES is now prepared to give financial assistance in this area of work. The Education Support Grants, introduced in 1985, allocated £980,000 to category H: 'Pilot projects related to educational needs in a multi-ethnic society.'

Forty-one authorities submitted bids in this category and 26 of these were granted aid. The North Tyneside Authority was the only north-eastern authority to be given a grant, of £39,000 over a three-year period to enable it to establish and staff a multicultural resource centre. This centre is now operational and it is intended that it will form the foundation for all in-service work within the authority. The authority realizes that it will be necessary to use the expertise available in the higher education sector, and Sunderland Polytechnic is to mount a diploma course in multicultural education at this centre in September 1987. Ten teachers from my own authority are currently following the Royal Society of Arts course 'English as a Second Language in the Multicultural Classroom', which is being offered by the University of Newcastle in conjunction with the Newcastle and North Tyneside authorities.

In November 1985 the In-Service Teacher Training Grants Scheme (DES Circular 3/85) added two additional priority areas to its original list of five. One of these was 'training concerned with the need to respond to ethnic diversity as identified in the Swann Report': it was proposed that £680,000 be made available for this purpose in 1986 – 87. Grants of this nature are very welcome, although it can be argued that they are still woefully inadequate for the task in hand.

Another area of funding which many local authorities are able to utilize is available from the Home Office, under section 11 of the Local Government Act 1966. Although the criterion for qualification for such a grant was changed in 1982 to one where it was not necessary to have 2 per cent of ethnic minority population within an authority to qualify, there is still a requirement to have 'substantial' numbers of such residents. Repeated applications from both North and South Tyneside were rejected on this criterion. Happily, in December 1985, North Tyneside was successful in its bid for funding for four staff to teach English as a second language. The implication is that section 11 funding is still intended to meet the immediate perceived needs of ethnic minority children within an area and is not intended to support 'education for all'.

My response to Swann, representing as I do almost an all-white area, is to concentrate on the need to educate, as Swann suggests, 'all children, all staff, to an understanding of the shared values of our society as a whole, as well as to an appreciation of the diversity of lifestyles and cultural, religious and linguistic backgrounds which make up this society and the wider world'. I have not discussed the authority's need to respond to the specific requirements of its minority groups in such areas as community language teaching and maintenance, and support for both children and adults in English language.

In my authority I feel that much of our work would have progressed without any Swann Report. What Swann has done in my opinion, however, is to give a good housekeeping seal of approval to the initiatives undertaken by many individuals and some local authorities in the field of multicultural education. It has produced much comment. With newspaper coverage, articles in such periodicals as *Education*, the *Times Educational Supplement* and publications from the Commission for Racial Equality, NAME and the Runnymede Trust, it has alerted many educationists to the need for action in their authorities. Its recommendations can be used both as a yardstick and as a lever in the pursuit of awareness raising and curriculum change to reflect the diversity and importance of the ethnic mix within society. Even without a single conference, a single debate, its very existence would have given credence to all within LEAs who wish to pursue a multicultural education policy.

References

BYRNE, D. (1977). 'The Arab Riots in South Shields', *Race and Class*, XVIII, 3.

DORN, A. and TROYNA, B. (1981). *Multi-Racial Education and the Politics of Decision-Making*. Birmingham: SSRC Unit of Ethnic Relations.

HUSBAND, C. (1982). *Race in Britain* London: Hutchinson.

MULLARD, C. (1982). 'Multiracial education in Britain: from assimilation to cultural pluralism'. In: TIERNEY, J. (Ed) *Race, Migration and Schooling*. Eastbourne: Holt, Saunders.

RICHARDSON, R. (1983). 'Worth the paper it's written on', *Issues*, (Autumn).

APPENDIX I

A Policy Statement

The Race Relations Act 1976 requires Local Authorities to carry out their various functions with 'due regard to the need

a) to eliminate unlawful discrimination;
b) to promote equality of opportunity and good relations between persons of different racial groups'.

The North Tyneside Education Committee welcomes this obligation and identifies the following aims as its declared policy in fulfilment of this obligation.

The North Tyneside Education Committee is convinced of the strength and inherent richness offered by cultural diversity. It seeks:

1. That, within all of its educational institutions, there shall be equality of educational opportunity for all individuals regardless of race, nationality or religion.
2. That the content and scope of the curriculum and the nature of teaching materials shall reflect the multicultural nature of both British society and the world.
3. That the ethos of each educational institution shall foster attitudes, relationships and habits through which may develop a respect and understanding of others of whatever national, racial, religious or cultural origin.

B Guidelines

1. The Director of Education will seek to collect and make available to Schools and Colleges information relating to the cultural and religious background of ethnic minorities.

Contacts with representatives of locally based ethnic minority groups will be made. Schools should, themselves, collect appropriate information to increase their store of knowledge and foster, through the curriculum, a greater understanding of the needs and values of ethnic minorities.

2. Schools and Colleges should collect and make available, where appropriate, basic information on ethnic minority pupils so that support may be given. This may include, for example, the identification of:

   a) those children where the language spoken at home is not English, together with the language spoken;
   b) those children who may have special dietary needs;
   c) those children who may need to recognize particular religious festivals during the school year;
   d) those children in need of support with English as a second language;
   e) those children who need to observe particular customs of dress.

3. The Authority will seek to further develop in-service training in Multicultural Education. The programme will seek to involve as many teachers as possible and school-based programmes will be developed.

4. The Authority will produce information in translation for ethnic minority parents and children. Initially this information will be concerned to introduce parents to the nature of the education system as it operates in North Tyneside.

5. Schools and Colleges may become aware of ethnic minority families who are experiencing social, educational or housing difficulties which may be compounded by language problems. In such cases, and where it is deemed necessary, Schools should seek professional advice from the appropriate Departments.

6. This Authority will continue to consult with ethnic minority communities so that their views can be made known to Schools, Colleges and Officers and to the appropriate Committees.

7. Teachers in all Schools and Colleges should examine the

literature available to pupils so that they are aware of those works which contain intentional or unintentional prejudice and can therefore discard or identify this material and use it in lessons as appropriate.

8.   This Authority has an agreed statement of policy for the School Curriculum 5–16. In accordance with Circular 6/81, issued by the Secretary of State, governors, teachers and all concerned need to set out in writing the aims which they pursue through the organization of the curriculum and in teaching programmes and should assess regularly how far the curriculum – in Schools as a whole and for individual pupils – matches the stated aims.

As part of that procedure, each School shall examine this Authority's multicultural education policy, state its aims in relation to multicultural education and shall develop its own policy statement on multicultural education designed to meet the particular needs of that School, which should be monitored annually.

The Authority recognizes that there may be need for detailed guidance on curricular matters and will give support through its Advisory Service with such matters. It will also seek to develop, in association with the Community Relations Council and other Tyne and Wear Local Education Authorities, detailed guidelines on these and other matters related to multicultural education.

9.   The Authority will continue to seek to meet the needs of ethnic minority children and adults who need help with English as a second language.

10.   This Authority will seek to support those ethnic minority groups who wish to undertake mother tongue teaching.

11.   The Authority will continue to meet the particular needs of ethnic minority pre-schoolchildren as part of its pre-school policy.

12.   Schools and Colleges should actively discourage racism. Incidents of a racist nature should be reported to the Director of Education. (See Note A.)

13.   Graffiti should be removed swiftly and the Authority will seek to continue the provision of proprietary graffiti removal materials. Where necessary, Schools and Colleges should seek help from the anti-graffiti squad.

Note A   Incidents of racial abuse would include:

1) verbal abuse;
2) racist graffiti;
3) physical abuse.

Schools would be expected to keep a record of such incidents and devise strategies for dealing with them.

WINIFRED MOULD'S COMMENTS

Following the production of an authority and of school policy statements, how should the LEA proceed?

Do we:

1. Get people like myself into schools to talk with staff and students about the nature of disadvantage, discrimination and racism in society, and attempt with them to examine the reasons for such inequalities?

2. Do we organize in-service work among groups of specialist subject-oriented teachers? Do we close the school either for a day or early, and effect a whole-school approach, and in this way reach those who support such initiatives as well as the doubting Thomases, the indifferents and the sceptics?

3. Do we attempt to allocate sums of money to schools, so that they can begin to purchase materials which we believe are multicultural? Where does this money come from?

4. Do we arrange working groups of teachers to produce non-racist materials and 'packs' which can then be used throughout the authority?

5. Do we invite representatives from minority groups into the schools and colleges to talk about their beliefs, their life-styles?

6. Do we offer in-service days and conferences when we look at such things as black women writers, or a study of Rangoli, Paisley and Willow patterns in art?

7. Do we arrange visits, exchanges or cross-communication with schools in dissimilar areas to our own – to rural schools and to schools with high-density minority representatives?

8. Do we include 'multicultural' questions at all teaching and perhaps also non-teaching interviews within the authority?

9. Do we look to the experiences of other LEAs and develop the strategies and materials they used – benefiting from both their successes and failures?

10. Do we arrange book and artefact exhibitions which can also be transported into the schools?
11. Do we ask school governors to discuss multicultural education at their regular meetings and provide someone from the authority to help them in their deliberations?
12. Do we involve parents in what we are attempting to do? How?
13. Do we positively attempt to employ black members of staff within the educational establishments?
14. Do we devise guidelines for schools to deal quickly and effectively with racist incidences?
15. Do we video pupil–teacher interaction in classrooms and later examine it for both incidences of racism and also of good practice?
16. Do we appoint a member of staff to be specifically responsible for multicultural education within a school or educational institution to act as a catalyst and as a referral? If so, do we ensure that that person is of sufficiently high status?
17. Do we second teachers from mainstream schooling for a period of two to three years to promote multicultural education?
18. Do we expect that all newly qualified teachers will have had training in multicultural education in their initial teaching training either as a module or as a philosophy which permeates their work? If not, do we contact the colleges of education and ask them to make such provision?
19. Do we contact all newly appointed members of staff and inform them of our policies with regard to multicultural education?
20. Are we aware that non-teaching staff need to be involved?

In the above 20 questions not one relates to the specific needs of some minority children. These would need another discussion paper.

It has been suggested that resources are relatively unimportant. I would refute that statement. Without them, – and here I am referring to the resources of time, money and personnel – we are severely limited in what we can attempt to do. Even if it is only a small carrot that we can dangle before schools, it is more likely to produce movement than no carrot at all.

5 Changing Attitudes: Prejudice and the Schools

James Lynch

One of the major ungrasped nettles of multicultural education in the UK has been the issue of how schools and teachers may undertake the task of systematically and rationally teaching for prejudice reduction and elimination. While sporadic forays into this territory have been made recently in the form of racism awareness training, there is nothing like the extensive literature on teaching to correct for prejudice which exists in the USA. Based on both empirical and conceptual research, the American literature has accumulated over more than half a century into a body of knowledge and experience, in many cases systematically evaluated and replicated, which cannot be ignored by those seeking to achieve similar objectives elsewhere. Yet in the isolated and discontinuous style which has tended to typify British efforts in this field, the vast potential of this literature has been largely ignored in favour of often more primitive and less well-grounded approaches, sometimes of a hortatory or polemical kind. The result of this neglect has been either an almost total disregard for the school's role in combating prejudice and discrimination or, on the other hand, short-term, spasmodic attempts at tackling particular prejudices in isolation and by methods which have been at best uninformed, at worst educationally dubious, attempts at indoctrination. Such efforts have usually remained unevaluated for their efficacy as for their other effects.

Yet culturally diverse societies inevitably and continually generate interpersonal and intergroup prejudices which, unchecked, may lead to bigotry, hostility, discrimination and even violence. For a culturally diverse society embraces a multiplicity of differing socialization and enculturation processes in the primary agencies of family and immediate community, which may be generative of predispositions to think, believe and act in ways which sharply diverge from those of other groups and are, in some cases, inimical to the values and norms of a pluralist democracy. So many children will enter school with prejudices which, unless 'evened out' by the school, will be reinforced by the wider society and, in turn, will influence the ambience of the school and its culture. Thus schools cannot remain neutral, for to do so would be to sanction the beliefs and behaviour which are hostile to, and sometimes destructive of, the moral base of a humane, democratic society which values human rights, freedom from irrational discrimination and a pluralism of legitimate cultures (Lynch, 1987).

Multicultural education in the UK, however, has consistently failed to take on board this important universal function, preferring instead to aim for soft targets such as folkloric content in the curriculum or the asserted need of some minority groups for improved self-images. Both of these goals may of course be highly laudable and desirable components of an overall approach to multicultural education, but they are far from being the whole story. They are, in other words, necessary but not sufficient, for they need to be integrated as part of a coherent and holistic commitment addressing both the special needs of some children and the common needs of all. For example, it is surely obvious that in so far as and for as long as policies to combat prejudice are focused on the special needs of black pupils alone, they are unlikely to alter radically or improve the racist attitudes present and active among the majority population, not least in the socially dominant groups. At the very least, the Swann Report seems to have placed that recognition firmly on the agenda. The corollary of that step is that until such a time as racism is accepted as an explicator of the problems of victimized groups, progress in formulating and legitimating more coherent and effective strategies in education as in the broader society on the basis of multi-factor explanations is likely to prove elusive and the multicultural rhetoricians will continue to have a field-day.

So in this paper I want to imagine that simplistic and uni-causal explanations of differential educational attainment have been discarded, and that accepting the role that racism may play in influencing the life-chances of visible minorities (and sexism and credism in marring the life-chances of those and other groups as well), schools have been given the explicit task of teaching to correct for prejudiced attitudes and beliefs. I want to ask the question of how multicultural education may build on what already exists and support the development of deliberate, systematic learning strategies and a school ethos which may reduce and if possible eradicate undesirable social attitudes and behaviour. In other words, and on the basis of our admittedly limited knowledge of how to correct for prejudice, what guidance and support may be given to teachers, to enable them to extend the criteria by which they judge their professional effectiveness so as to include prejudice reduction? I am of course aware that such a commitment implies that schools and teachers are able to make professional judgements on the basis of rational criteria about what is right and what is wrong in a multicultural society, educational system and school. In turn, that competence implies an acceptance of the essentially moral nature of a teacher's professional role. In a democracy, too, the criteria underlying such decisions must of course be subject to discourse involving all legitimate cultural groups.

First however, what do we mean by prejudice? In its literal sense prejudice is the holding of a belief or opinion without adequate rational grounds or in the face of rational evidence to the contrary. As Bethlehem (1985) points out, such prejudice may focus on persons or things; it may be positive or negative in a formal sense. It is not a priori a hostile or negative opinion or belief, for we may be prejudiced *for* a person or thing as well as against them. Moreover, in this sense we all have prejudices. So the question arises of which prejudices must be addressed by teachers and schools, how and when. The answer is by no means simple or straightforward.

As teachers, we expect children to make discriminations, ranging from placing objects into sets, thus categorizing them, to differentiating between discriminable stimuli and alternative good and bad behaviour. We do not expect them to categorize as identical phenomena where rational grounds exist for discrimination. We also expect them to be able to learn how to generalize from specific evidence, interpreting accurately and fairly. Thus the task of educators is to enable children to achieve the rational bases, information, techniques, views and strategies which will make it possible for them to categorize and generalize correctly on the basis of rational evidence and procedures, while avoiding stereotypical representations and prejudiced beliefs and resisting invitations to prejudiced attitudes and behaviour, deriving from labels such as ethnic origin, race, sex, class and creed. Teachers thus expect children to make some legitimate discriminations, while avoiding and resisting others, for which there is no rational evidence.

Here the moral dimension of education is important, for it is those prejudices which offend against the moral bases of a multicultural society and infringe human rights and dignity which need to be 'cooled out' by schools, for these are the ones which are destructive of the very fabric of society. That imperative for the school to act is accentuated when the preconceived and stereotypical representation of a particular group or individual may motivate actions and behaviour which cause them injustice and even harm. In sum, schools are necessarily involved in a culturally diverse society in the rational and moral task of educating children out of negative attitudes and behaviour and of initiating them into morally acceptable attitudes and behaviour, congruent with the basic ethic of a multicultural society and its commitment to human rights and freedoms. Such a task is both complex and demanding and it necessitates a continual and coherent reinforcement throughout the school life of the child and the extension of the currently existing skills and expertise of many teachers.

I accept of course that there are weaknesses with the formulation that I have introduced. First, far from combating stereotypes and prejudices, education, colluding with other agencies such as the media, may be argued to propagate and reinforce them whether in the field of sex stereotyping, ethnic pride, racial derivation, social status or linguistic register. Indeed, there are those who argue convincingly that social class and religious categorization and hierarchization is fundamental to the very social organization, political structure and educational system. Secondly, in an era of increasing instrumental regulation of human behaviour in Western societies as opposed to the former theological one, it is difficult but by no means impossible to achieve agreement on the basic ethic of a multicultural society which would enable us to identify what prejudices to counter and why. Can, for example, education for national pride be a source of prejudice against other ethnic groups? Can religious education foster inter-group bigotry, rivalry, hostility and even violence? We would all recognize that the answer to these two questions can be a positive one.

For this reason, fundamental changes are needed in the wider society as in the school, if those prejudices are to be overcome which are destructive of the very fabric of society. Major legal and political changes are certainly needed, for education can only solve educational problems. In such a co-ordinated initiative, however, the schools and individual teachers do have an important role to play, for they are the ones who daily have to make the decisions about what constitutes moral behaviour in a multicultural society. For the decision about what prejudice to tackle in schools, and how and when, derives directly from what is good and bad, acceptable and unacceptable, positive and negative in a multicultural society (Lynch, 1983, 1986, 1987).

There are many ways in which teachers may show their commitment to prejudice reduction and elimination but, most important, they may demonstrate it in their everyday lives and teaching. Schools too may show their commitment to prejudice reduction by developing a democratic ethos, manifesting a commitment to delivering equity for all pupils and structuring their work on the basis of democratic values such as human justice, freedom and dignity. Both schools and teachers need to empower their pupils actively to pursue democratic values and to combat prejudice. But in order to do so, teachers and schools themselves have to be empowered not with well-worn technocratic mechanisms for the solution of hand-me-down issues, but towards a new critical intellectual relationship with their communities, with society and with the ends of education in a democratic society, which really appreciates cultural diversity through the way that it structures its discourse. As Aronowitz and Giroux have argued (1985a, 1985b), the role of the teacher needs to become that of the transformative intellectual, involved in the critical political discourse about ends as well as means in the pursuit of more just social relations and a more equitable society, which excludes current prejudices such as racism, sexism, credism and classism. The problem with that formulation is that as legitimation crises in the broader society have accentuated, schools and teachers have increasingly been allocated an 'NCO' role as a technical arm of minor state apparatuses, by dominant groups and governments. Such a relegation has implied an almost exclusive concern with technical means rather than the changing ends of education and an increasing unwillingness to recognize that teachers are part of the power political structure and that they work in the context of economic and ideological conditions. They are thus part of, not apart from, the overall discourse concerning legitimate ends for a culturally diverse society which implements as well as declares democratic values. Schools and teachers are thus neither totally dominated by the social system nor totally autonomous from it, but participants in an arena for discourse about educational ends and means.

One final point before I proceed to the kinds of strategy which may be adopted by schools to achieve attitudes and behaviour which do not negatively discriminate on the basis of race, sex, ethnic origins and creed: that is, what a multicultural society is ultimately concerned with is acceptable behaviour – and it is the task of education to provide for the making of individual and group judgements to support that. To achieve that goal, education has to tackle the covert motivators of discriminatory behaviour by concentrating on what is rationally justifiable acceptable behaviour within our society. Here there are contrary views. Some argue that if the behaviour is changed, the beliefs will also change. Others assert that the values and attitudes have to be changed, so that behaviour will follow. To my mind, teaching for both goals is also tenable and can be effective, provided that cognitive, affective and behavioural dimensions are taken into account. But how? Let me discuss briefly some of the pedagogical work which has attempted to address that task and let us see if it is possible to draw out some guiding principles.

As I have stated earlier in this paper, most of the work in the field of prejudice reduction has been conducted in the USA over the past half-century. There is, however, a small amount of pioneer work in the UK on which we can draw. The work of Stenhouse in the early 1970s, for example, will be well known to many educationists. It remains unique in the UK in its innovatory contribution to the development of a multicultural education aimed at enhancing the rational judgement of those being educated. In a book published after his untimely death Stenhouse

et al. (1982) set out what he called a number of researchers'
speculations, and I have summarized some of these as offering a
direct contribution to practical initiatives which need to be borne
in mind in the development of strategies for prejudice reduction
(Lynch, 1986). Included are the following points, which I have
paraphrased and re-written for this paper:

1. Direct teaching to correct for negative racial attitudes can
   result in positive gains.
2. Strategies compatible with the context and the skills of
   teachers who are involved are more likely to be successful.
3. The value of 'open-mindedness' is likely to transfer from
   the discussion of one controversial issue into another.
4. The results of such gains are likely to be non-persistent
   without reinforcement.
5. Where the teaching/learning strategies include an appeal
   to the judgement of participants, they may in some cases
   result in regression in an undesired direction.
6. In the face of racism there is a need for collegiality of
   decision.
7. Only as part of broader social policies and interests is it
   likely that tackling racism in the school will be successful.

I am not suggesting that each of the above principles is precisely as
formulated by Stenhouse, but rather attempting to give provisional guiding principles which emerged for me from his work. If
we then add to these principles others deriving from the work of
scholars and educators in the UK and elsewhere, it is possible to
commence construction, brick by brick, of a pedagogy of multicultural education which comes to grips with issues of how to tackle
prejudice reduction and to correct for racism, sexism, classism and
credism.

If we look at the work of Jeffcoate (1976, 1979a, 1979b), we can
find a series of cognitive and affective objectives for a multicultural and multiracial curriculum which might be able to address
issues of prejudice reduction. As his work has been amended by
Cohen and Manion (1983) and Lynch (1986), it includes not only
cognitive skills (it is important for cognitive knowledge to be
acquired in order to correct for misinformation), but also
embraces affective attitudes, values and emotional sets. This is an

important contribution to our discussion of prejudice reduction because it implies a recognition that prejudice comprises emotionality and emotional dimensions as well as cognitive ones, and that any curriculum, to be effective, must include both. Of course we might add that there is also a conative or behavioural dimension, which equally is often neglected. So from his work emerge two further principles to add to our catalogue of proposed good practice:

8.   Educational strategies for prejudice reduction must include teaching for cognitive gains, for example, to correct for misinformation.
9.   Prejudice reduction must include affective and behavioural objectives as well as cognitive ones.

Walkling (1980) raises basic ethical issues concerning the principles for the selection of the content of a multicultural curriculum which are of direct assistance to us in making decisions about teaching/learning strategies to correct for prejudice. His work responds to the much repeated question of the multicultural nihilists about who should decide. He is concerned with how fair and just decisions about what should be included in the curriculum may be made, the procedures that might be involved and the kinds of purpose which might be addressed. Drawing up a series of continua between tolerance and selection in the case of content; relativism and absolutism in the case of procedures; and transition and transformation in the case of purposes, he constructs a typology which identifies the complexity of decisions involved, but also clarifies the decisions which have to be made. Using his terms, decisions about prejudice reduction are likely to address transformational goals on the basis of a selection from the overall culture of the nation state, including minority cultures but not embracing the totality, and to tend to relativism in the procedures to be adopted. Thus we may say that educational strategies for prejudice reduction must recognize certain fundamental principles and that one of these is the need for such principles to be subject to discourse in their implementation: that discourse to include all legitimate cultural interests. Schools, being part of the structure of the nation state, will also need to adopt democratic practice in their structure and in their teaching. A democratic school and classroom atmosphere is thus a further necessity for educational strategies to correct for prejudiced attitudes.

If we now turn across the Atlantic to the work of Banks in the USA, we find a commitment to holistic strategies as the basis for prejudice reduction. Banks calls for the permeation of the whole-school environment, its purposes, values and ethos, by means of measures which are comprehensive in scope and sequence. He envisages a process of cultural reciprocity between and among teachers and pupils, encouraged by positive inter-ethnic interactions, including the close involvement of the local community (Banks, 1981, 1982, 1984). So basing our principles on Bank's work, we may say:

10. The strategies must be holistic and include the total school environment.
11. There must be a permeation of the purposes, values and attitudes of multiculturalism into every facet of the school's functioning.
12. The measures must be comprehensive in scope and sequence.
13. This will necessitate multi-disciplinary approaches and multi-directionality in purposes.
14. The principles involved will encompass and embrace mutual and multiple acculturation of pupil and teacher by each other in a process of cultural reciprocity.
15. Approaches must include positive multi-ethnic interactions with significant others.
16. The staff composition must reflect ethnic pluralism.
17. Learning styles must take account of the ethnic pluralism of the school.
18. Continuous efforts are needed including systematic reinforcement.
19. Teaching/learning approaches need to address both decision-making and social-actioning competencies.
20. The curriculum must aim to strengthen the intercultural competence of the pupils.
21. Maximum use needs to be made of the resources and skills of the local community.
22. The holistic strategy must include particular attention to assessment and evaluation.

While I am not proposing that such tentative principles as I have listed above represent as yet a fully developed middle-range theory, or series of middle-range theories, they do represent a limited set of assumptions and presuppositions from which specific principles of professional action may be derived and subjected to confirmation by empirical investigation, and from which valid generalizations may be made in a logically consistent way. We are, in other words, already in a position to construct an interrelated series of provisional middle-range theories, which could effectively guide the implementation of teaching/learning strategies to correct for prejudice, the evaluation of those strategies and their consequent empirical verification and improvement. So the benchmarks for effective educational action in the schools addressing the goal of prejudice reduction are available, if only we would have regard to them and stop trying to reinvent the wheel with stone-age tools. The principles, identified above, could be further refined and added to by taking account of some of the more speculative and less thoroughly grounded work. From the series of BBC programmes focused on the issue of multicultural education, issues concerned with staff development lead us to realize that any strategy for the introduction of prejudice reduction teaching must have at its core an effective staff development strategy, starting where the teachers 'are now' with their current attitudes and knowledge, their current professional behaviour and professional criteria. It must surely include the sensitive exploration of the phenomenon of institutional racism and pupils' and teachers' feelings and experiences of it.

Such principles must, however, be seen in the context of research and writing in the field of prejudice acquisition and reduction, or there is a strong possibility of naïve action leading to damage and perhaps even increasing unhealthy social attitudes and practices. There are basically four domains of research and writing on these areas, overlapping but emphasizing respectively personality, social structure, culture and environment. These four explanatory domains have leapfrogged each other in their development over the past 50 years and it is probably the case that any satisfactory middle-range theory will have to take into account all of them. Unfortunately, I do not have the space here to discuss the four domains in detail (see Lynch, 1987); but I do want to state clearly what I mean by prejudice reduction. For me, it is a deliberate and systematic process which aims, by means of coherent and sustained educational and broader social strategies, policies and practices, to enable individuals and groups to re-orient their beliefs and behaviour in such a way that their predispositions to negatively discriminate are attenuated or eradicated. It is an essentially moral, rational and educational process, carried out according to principles appropriate to the values of a democratic society, and it eschews coercion and indoctrination.

One further point is necessary before I move on briefly to discuss possible change strategies which have been adopted and to propose a brief list of tentative and provisional principles. As Merton (1976) has pointed out, it is quite possible for a person who is not him/herself prejudiced to be a discriminator. The circumambient values of the institution or society may exercise an influence which produces in the non-prejudiced, well-intentioned person false stereotypes or even, on occasions, merely silence, either of which may enhance and facilitate their perpetration of discrimination on the basis of race, sex, class or creed. It is therefore important for strategies of prejudice reduction to bear in mind these major dimensions of prejudice: individual, structural, cultural and environmental, and to incorporate this insight into the design of pedagogical initiatives to correct for prejudice.

Turning now to some of the change strategies of which we have details, and which may provide nodal points for the development of more overarching approaches to the eradication of prejudice, we are faced with a wide variety of disparate, unconnected and non-continuous approaches, including the matching of change strategies and pedagogical principles; strategies at pre-school level; teaching through drama; attempts at change by discourse; role-playing and simulation exercises; the production of materials and packs; the encouragement of teachers to study their own practice and expand the criteria for the judgement of their own professional actions and practices; and attempts to introduce multicultural education to correct for prejudice by predominantly cognitive means, both in schools and in teacher education. Gay (1982) cautions that education needs to aim at higher levels of intellectual functioning and social and moral perspective-taking, for there is evidence that those who achieve these higher levels are likely to be involved in prejudiced social behaviour.

While a number of academics (including Gibson, Williams, Lynch and others) have attempted to draw maps of these initiatives, we have as yet no complete 'cartographical' survey of the initiatives which have been taken so far let alone systematic and scientific theories for prejudice reduction. We do, however, have overviews of the literature and evaluations of some of the teaching techniques. I have identified and summarized elsewhere (Lynch, 1987) some of the core literature on prejudice reduction in schools and proposed 12 major teaching approaches out of which teachers may construct their own integrated teaching strategy. These 12 approaches include direct teaching; principle-testing and values education; inter-ethnic contact; drama and simulation; moral education; case studies; co-operative groupwork; coaching; discourse; coalition formation; materials approaches; and awareness training. In each case I have looked at the evidence for the efficacy of the particular approach, its weaknesses and its interdependence with the other approaches, and with the overall democratic classroom ethos and school climate. I have argued that integration of the different approaches into the personal teaching style of the educator may be expected to lead to cognitive, affective and behavioural gains, higher self-esteem for all pupils, an increased sense of personal efficacy and lower levels of prejudice and learning anxiety as well as improved academic performance and intellectual attainment.

If I am correct in my interpretation of the available evidence, then we already have available to us the means whereby teachers and schools may address successfully the task of prejudice reduction. What is lacking is the political will and the educational initiative. Moreover, the interesting thing about these educational strategies and teaching/learning approaches is the large measure of overlap which they enjoy with the characteristic components of effective schools according to research on both sides of the Atlantic (Kyle, 1985; US Department of Education, 1986; HMI, 1977; Rutter *et al.*, 1979). Cumulatively the force of such research and writing is sufficient to persuade us that a school can develop a good ethos, serving both intellectual and social dimensions of its work and that each facet of the ethos will support the other: academic and intellectual achievement and improved social relations and attitudes. As I have argued in detail elsewhere, academic attainment does not have to take a 'back seat' to improved social relations and attitudes (Crain, Mahard and Narat, 1982; Slavin *et al.*, 1985).

So prejudice reduction can give a double bonus in school and classroom, provided that it is organized according to specific principles. What those principles are emerges clearly in the case of some teaching/learning strategies and less clearly in the case of others, but more eloquently than ignorance in the case of all. We already have a number of interconnected middle-range assumptions on which prejudice reduction may be based with regard to such approaches as inter-ethnic contact (Allport, 1954), co-operative groupwork (Johnson *et al.*, 1981; Sharan *et al.*, 1985), moral education (Kohlberg, 1984), principle testing (Kehoe, 1984a, 1984b, 1984c) and coaching and expectation training (Stephan, 1985; Cohen, Lockheed and Lohman, 1976), so why not use them?

The upshot of the brief excursion here is no more than a series of tentative and provisional reflections, identifying possible guiding principles for the establishment of policies of multicultural education by teachers in schools and a pathway to possible middle-way theories for pedagogical approaches to teachers in schools. There is much work still to be done, but I would summarize the major points which I have made in this paper as the following imperatives:

1. A recognition of the central role of staff development, starting from where teachers are now and including their own study of their own practice.
2. The need for teachers to extend the criteria by which they judge their own practice and to extend their frame of reference for such judgement.
3. The need for inclusive, comprehensive, systematic, continuous and holistic school approaches.
4. Multi-dimensional and inter-disciplinary pedagogical approaches are necessary, including interconnected and coherent phases of reinforcement, addressing higher levels of mental functioning.
5. Pedagogical initiatives need to be reflective of the cultural, racial and linguistic biography of the school and society.
6. Strategies need to be true to the underlying ethical principles which may be derived either from philosophical

speculation or from international agreements and covenants and national legislation.

7. Multicultural education for prejudice reduction must address cognitive, affective and conative dimensions and objectives.

8. Multicultural education aiming at prejudice reduction must include well-constructed inter-ethnic interactions, designed according to the principles identified in the literature.

9. Holistic strategies must include all aspects of the school, including its assessment and evaluation policies.

10. Democratic values and educational procedures inevitably limit and define the policies and strategies available.

11. Social-actioning skills are an essential part of the basics of education for prejudice reduction.

12. A democratic, supportive and well-ordered school and classroom ethos are essential prerequisites for teaching/ learning approaches to correct for prejudice.

13. The pedagogical approaches for prejudice reduction should be constructed to consciously take account of the most recent research and literature in the field.

14. Such approaches demand the recognition of the role of teachers as transformative intellectuals (Aronowitz and Giroux, 1985a, 1985b).

15. Inter-learning is an essential prerequisite to prejudice reduction.

Clearly, it follows from what I have said that manifestations of racial discrimination and other prejudiced behaviour on the part of pupils and/or teachers should be seen as disciplinary offences and treated accordingly on the basis of an explicit policy and delivery statement. It is important that all teachers recognize that racist behaviour cannot and will not be tolerated in a multicultural school, for it is incompatible with the ethics of that institution and its society. While the difficulties should not be underestimated (see e.g. Troyna and Ball, 1985), as part of its overall strategy each school needs to draw up a delivery document which will also include guidelines for teachers on how to react to manifestations of racism and prejudice in their own schools and classroom. The delivery will need to be collegially supported and organically implemented and evaluated, and that represents a major – but not insuperable, – task of institution-based INSET. None of us can claim that we are adequately prepared for the complexity of the task of implementing multicultural education in a manner which will achieve prejudice reduction and, hopefully, eradication. But we have enough to start the process. Without staff development, however, there can be no effective education for prejudice reduction – and without such an education the outlook for our schools, society and children could be very bleak indeed.

Note

I am grateful to my colleague, Barry Troyna, for his constructive comments on an early draft of this paper.

References

ALLPORT, G.W. (1954). *The Nature of Prejudice*. New York: Addison-Wesley.

ARONOWITZ, S. and GIROUX, H.A. (1985a). 'Radical education and transformative intellectuals', *Canadian Journal of Political and Social Theory*, 99, 3, pp.48–63.

ARONOWITZ, S. and GIROUX, H.A. (1985b). *Education under Siege*. South Hadley, Mass.: Bergin and Harvey.

BANKS, J.A. (1981). *Multiethnic Education: Theory and Practice*. Boston, Mass.: Allyn and Bacon.

BANKS, J.A. (1982). Reducing Prejudice in Students: Theory, Research and Strategies. Paper presented at the Kamloops Spring Institute for Teacher Education, Faculty of Education, Simon Fraser University, Burnaby, British Columbia, 3 Feb.

BANKS, J.A. (1984). *Teaching Strategies for Ethnic Studies*. Boston, Mass.: Allyn and Bacon.

BETHLEHEM, D.W. (1985). *A Social Psychology of Prejudice*. London: Croom Helm.

COHEN, E.G., LOCKHEED, M.E. and LOHMAN, M.R. (1976). 'The Centre for Interracial Co-operation: a field experiment', *Sociology of Education*, 49, pp.47–58.

COHEN, L. and MANION, L. (1983). *Multicultural Classrooms.* London: Croom Helm.

CRAIN, R., MAHARD, R. and NARAT, R. (1982). *Making Desegregation Work.* Cambridge, Mass: Ballinger.

GAY, G. (1982). 'Developmental prerequisites for multicultural education in the social studies'. In: ROSENZWEIG, L.W. (Ed) *Developmental Perspectives in the Social Studies.* Bulletin 66. Washington, DC: National Council for the Social Studies.

HMI (1977). *Ten Good Schools: a Secondary School Enquiry.* London: HMSO.

JEFFCOATE, R. (1976). 'Curriculum planning in multiracial education', *Educational Research,* 18,3, pp.192–200.

JEFFCOATE, R. (1979a). 'A multi-cultural curriculum: beyond the orthodoxy', *Trends in Education,* Vol. 4, pp.8–12.

JEFFCOATE, R. (1979b). *Positive Image: Towards a Multiracial Curriculum.* London: Chameleon.

JOHNSON, D.W., MARIYAMA, G., JOHNSON, D., NELSON, D. and SKON, L. (1981). 'The effects of co-operative, competitive and individual goal structures on achievement: a meta-analysis', *Psychological Bulletin ,* 89, pp.47–62.

KEHOE, J.W. (1984a). *A Handbook for Enhancing the Multicultural Climate of the School.* Vancouver, B.C.: University of British Columbia.

KEHOE, J.W. (1984b). *Multicultural Canada: Consideration for Schools, Teachers and Curriculum.* Vancouver, B.C.: University of British Columbia.

KEHOE, J.W. (1984c). *Achieving Cultural Diversity in Canadian Schools.* Cornwall, Ontario: Vesta.

KOHLBERG, L. (1984). *Essays on Moral Development.* San Francisco, Calif.: Harper and Row.

KYLE, R.A. (1985). *Reaching for Excellence: an Effective School Handbook.* Washington, DC: US Government Printing Office.

LYNCH, J. (1983). *The Multicultural Curriculum.* London: Batsford.

LYNCH, J. (1985). 'Human rights, racism and the multicultural curriculum', *Educational Review,* 37,2 (Summer).

LYNCH, J. (1986). *Multicultural Education: Principles and Practice.* London:Routledge and Kegan Paul.

LYNCH, J. (1987). *Prejudice Reduction and the Schools.* Eastbourne:Holt Saunders.

MILNER, D. (1983). *Children and Race Ten Years On*. London: Ward Lock Educational.

RUTTER, M. *et al.* (1979). *Fifteen Thousand Hours: Secondary Schools and their Effects on Children*. London:Open Books.

SHARAN, S. *et al.* (1985). 'Co-operative learning effects on ethnic relations in Israeli junior high school classrooms'. In: SLAVIN, R.E. *et al.* (Eds) *Learning to Co-operate: Co-operating to Learn*. New York: Plenum Press.

SLAVIN, R.E. *et al.* (Eds) (1985). *Learning to Co-operate: Co-operating to Learn*. New York: Plenum Press.

STENHOUSE, L. *et al.* (1982). *Teaching about Race Relations: Problems and Effects*. London: Routledge and Kegan Paul.

STEPHAN, W.G. (1985). 'Intergroup relations'. In: LINDZEY, G. and ARONSON, E. (Eds) *The Handbook of Social Psychology*. New York: Random House.

TAJFEL, H. (1981). 'Social stereotypes and social groups'. In: TURNER, J. and GILES, H. (Eds) *Intergroup Behaviour*. Chicago: University of Chicago Press.

TROYNA, B. and BALL, W. (1985). *Views from the Chalkface: School Responses to an LEA's Policy on Multiracial Education*. Coventry: University of Warwick.

TWITCHIN, J. and DEMUTH, S. (1985). *Multicultural Education*. London: BBC.

UNITED STATES DEPARTMENT OF EDUCATION (1986). *What Works: Research about Teaching and Learning*. Washington, DC: US Department of Education.

WALKLING, P. (1980). 'The idea of a multicultural curriculum', *Journal of Philosophy*, 14, 1, pp.87–95.

6 Understanding Multicultural/Anti-Racist Education for Practice

Carlton Duncan

It is true that blacks (the term is used to refer to anyone who is not regarded as white) came to this country in any significant numbers only after 1945 when, in response to Britain's call, large numbers of people came from the West Indies and the Indian sub-continent to fill vacancies which the British people themselves would not fill. The full-employment policies and associated rise in standard of living meant that the host labourforce could be selective in terms of employment prospects. The largely unskilled labourforce from overseas had to be turned to, and the lure of jobs and better pay made the British invitation attractive. It was to be expected that in a mainly chauvinistic world it would be the menfolk, in the main, who would come in answer to this invitation. Equally, it was to be expected that family ties would inevitably lead to additional immigration as the workers would send for their families to join them here.

This, however, does not mean that Britain became a multiracial society, as far as black people are concerned, for the first time following the end of the Second World War. On the contrary, considerable evidence does exist to show that there was a sizeable black presence from much earlier times. Granville Sharpe, in the 1700s, estimated that there were some 20,000 black people in Britain (1764). The Imperial War Museum and the RAF Museum at Hendon, in London, attract thousands of visitors each year, and any public librarian will tell you that the section on the history of the two World Wars is one of the best used in the library. Yet one aspect of both world wars seems to have been completely overlooked. That is, the part played in these dreadful conflicts by black people. All told, some 3½ million blacks fought on behalf of the UK if the figures from both wars are taken together.

It is all the more worrying to note that the British educational system made no serious response to accommodate very large numbers of black children which became a reality in schools in many parts of the country. This is so in spite of the fact that the black communities themselves recognized the need for a positive educational response, echoed this need loudly and indeed began active self-help organizations variously described as Saturday Schools, Evening Schools or Supplementary Schools in all parts of the country. Many of these late 1960s and 1970s arrangements are still in evidence today and are doing extremely well for the pupils for whom they cater.

When, at last, any official recognition of the need for some educational response to the black presence in the school eventually came, it took on board an assimilationist philosophy. Action had to be taken which would lead to the rapid absorption of these immigrants into the majority population. But there were obstacles to this. The popular view was that these immigrants could not speak English and many suffered 'culture shock'. It followed, therefore, that if educational provision concentrated on removing these barriers, assimilation would be expedited, so the logic ran. This position clearly had official support: 'From the beginning the major educational task is the teaching of English' (DES, 1965). As we know, special funding (Local Government Act, 1966, Section 11), was soon to be established which would assist local authorities and schools with the employment of teachers of English as a second language (E2L), so that these 'problem' children could be taught English, for the most part, in separate language centres.

It is, therefore, little wonder that black children and black people have since been seen as a problem, rather than for the positive contribution which they are without doubt capable of making towards the enrichment of British society. The assimilation was expected to be rapid. To this effect, it is worth noting that the special funding set up to assist this programme was applicable to immigrants of less than ten years' presence. Similarly, the statistical instrument (Form 7(i)) which assisted both the DES and local authorities in the counting of immigrant children, counted only children who were born of immigrants of less than ten years' presence. Sadly, much of this assimilationist practice still goes on in British education today. The language reception centres are still in evidence and the E2L arrangements have altered little.

Another major assimilationist response to immigrant children was to ensure that not too many found themselves in any one school. In Margaret Thatcher's language this would be to 'swamp' the others in the school. Consequently, the policy adopted by certain local authorities was one of busing black children (not the white children) to distant schools, so as to keep their numbers 30 per cent or less in the school. If we examine the official position on this matter, we see yet again the stigmatization of black children as 'problems':

> The presence of a high proportion of immigrant children in one class slows down the general routine of working and hampers the progress of the whole class, especially where the immigrants do not speak or write English fluently. This is clearly in itself undesirable and unfair to all the children in the class. (Commonwealth Immigrants Advisory Council, 1964)

This very closely resembles what follows (I wonder who copied from whom?):

> At no point in all this sound and fury does the plight of those white children who constitute the 'ethnic minority' in a growing number of inner-city schools merit even a mention. Yet their educational 'disadvantage' is now confirmed. It is no more than common sense that if a school contains a disproportionate number of children for whom English is a second language ... then academic standards are bound to suffer. (Honeyford, 1984)

This latter quote clearly shows that what was first written in 1964 lingers still, and in the minds of teachers to whom the care of young children are entrusted.

In 1963 the then Minister of Education clearly had 'busing' in mind when he said in the House of Commons:

If possible, it is desirable on education grounds that no one school should have more than 30 per cent immigrants ... I must regretfully tell the House that one school must be regarded now as irretrievably an immigrant school. The important thing to do is to prevent this happening elsewhere. (Hansard, 27 November 1984, vol. 685, 433–4)

All, therefore, would be done from the highest level downwards to ensure that the black child's moral values, manners, social behaviour, language, customs, practices, religion, and so on, would be assimilated rapidly into those of the white majority. It would not work, could not work and did not work. The Swann Report said of the assimilationist response to the black presence: 'above all the assimilationist approach seems to have recognized the existence of a single cultural criterion which was 'white', Christian and English speaking, and to have failed to acknowledge any wider implications of the changing nature of British society' (Swann, 1985, p.196).

This next quotation, taken from the Institute of Race Relations Report (1969), sums up well the assimilationist attempt rapidly to transform black children into something other than they were:

The whole question of the educational effect of dispersal schemes was given only cursory attention when the policy was first proposed. For some, the point of the policy was to make life easier for teachers in schools which would normally have large intakes of children of immigrants. For others, the policy was a way of preventing the development of 'all immigrant' schools which were *per se* undesirable. For still others, dispersal was an essential basis for cultural assimilation, including the learning of English ... Little or no thought had been devoted to a clear analysis of the nature and the extent of the educational needs of the immigrants. It was wrongly assumed that an influx of immigrant pupils into a school automatically hampered the chances of native English children in the school and that the children were competitors for the teacher's attention under all circumstances ... Official policy gave the accurate impression of having been devised under the pressure of circumstances and based on received ideas. Central to both was the concept that, as a result of the coming of immigrant pupils, the schools were changing for the worse ... The official dispersal policy, with its emphasis on preserving the normal routine of a school, was in a sense a Canute-like attempt, to prevent change. (p.288)

And the next clearly discernible response to the black presence might be described as the integrationist stage. More accurately, this might be described as that point in time when it was realized that the rapid assimilation was not happening and so white teachers had to make a concession. This concession amounted to a mushrooming of short in-service courses and trips to the West Indies and India for teachers to learn something of the life-style and culture of the 'immigrants'. The purpose of this was really no more than an exercise to ease and expedite the process of assimilation; HMI Eric Bolton puts it well:

Contrary to the assimilationist belief that, given English language fluency, the immigrant would disappear into the crowd, those arguing for integration claimed that a much more planned and detailed education and social programme needed to be undertaken if immigrants were to be able to integrate with the majority society. The emphasis was still upon integrating the minorities with the majority society and culture so that a culturally homogeneous society would be created. This meant that it was up to the minorities to change and adapt, and there was little or no pressure upon the majority society to modify or change its prevailing attitudes or practices. However, to enable integration to take place, it was argued that the majority society needed to be more aware of historical and cultural factors affecting different minorities. Knowledge and awareness would enable the majority society to make allowances for differences in lifestyle, culture and religion that might make it difficult for some immigrant groups to integrate with British society and would help to avoid the embarrassing mistakes that could arise from ignorance. (Bolton, 1979, p.4)

We see again that the emphasis is almost entirely upon the black pupils as immigrants from other countries rather than as an integral part of British society, and this was so even though an increasing number of these children were British-born second-generation children. It is easy, therefore, to account for much of the negative stereotypes of black people which persist still today.

The Swann Report's view of both the integrationist approach and that of the assimilationist is thus expressed: 'it is hardly surprising that we regard both the assimilationist and integrationist educational responses to the needs of ethnic minority pupils as, in retrospect, misguided and ill-founded' (Swann, 1985, p.198). What in fact was necessary, and is necessary, to save present and future generations of black children in the schools is a multicultural approach *in an anti-racist sense*. Too often we find schools where the fact that the music department has a set of steel drums, where Guru Nanak's birthday or Diwali or a West Indian evening of Blues and/or Reggae is celebrated or takes place occasionally is passed off as multicultural education. Multicultural education has its critics (Stone, 1981) but much of the criticisms result either from a misunderstanding of what it is or because, as defined, it amounts to nothing more than peripheral tinkering.

Multicultural education which is anti-racist based seeks equitable restructuring of power structures and the just redistribution of the power held. To the extent that education is a tool to power, it is necessary to concentrate efforts there. Rather than tinkering, we need to get right to the heart of everything that happens within the school.

Given the clear failure of the assimilationist and integrationist philosophies to get black education right, multicultural education in the sense defined above is seen as the answer. What, then does all this mean in reality? For practitioners a series of questions, beginning with 'Why multicultural education?', have to be answered.

Many researchers and official reports have shown that black pupils underachieve in British schools (Rampton Report, 1981). It is emerging, too, that a concomitant problem is that of misinformation via the school curriculum to all children with different effects on them depending on whether they are white or black. Let us recall some of the evidence pertaining to underachievement and the question of misinformation.

In 1963 a study by Brent LEA found the performance of black children was, on average, much lower than that of white children in reading, arithmetic and spelling.

In 1965 a study carried out by Vernon (1965) comparing black children in London and Hertfordshire showed similar results.

In 1966 the Inner London Education Authority researches noted dissatisfaction with the performance of black children as compared with white children of the same age within the local authority area.

In 1966 and 1968 Dr Little's studies of reading standards of nine-year-olds in the Inner London Education Authority showed that black children were performing less well at primary school than white children from the same social-economic backgrounds.

Further, section 11 of the 1966 Local Government Act provides special funds to local authorities (75 per cent of cost) to meet the special needs of ethnic minorities within their areas. It seems reasonable to conclude that from early days governments had cause for concern about the education of black children.

Indeed, in 1978 a study undertaken in the Redbridge Borough of London corroborated all that had gone before ('West Indian Pupils in Redbridge').

But the study which was responsible more than any other for arousing public consciousness was that of Bernard Coard (1971). After revealing that a disproportionately large number of West Indian children found their way to schools for the educationally sub-normal, he concluded:

> If the children of us immigrants were to get equal educational opportunities then in one generation there would be no large labour pool from under-developed countries, prepared to do the menial and unwanted jobs, in the economic system, at the lowest wages and in the worst housing; for our children armed with a good education, would demand the jobs and the social status that goes with such jobs – befitting their educational qualifications. This would be a very bad blow to Britain's 'Social Order' with its notions about the right place of the black man in relation to the white man in society. (Coard, 1971, p.35)

It was in this climate and around the same period that all three political parties considered the situation serious enough to set up an all-party Select Committee of the House of Commons to investigate issues pertaining to ethnic minorities. They reported in 1977, making a number of recommendations pertaining to education. One of these called upon the government of the day to set up 'as a matter of urgency a high level independent Inquiry' to find out why ethnic minorities were underachieving in schools. Hence the Rampton/Swann inquiries. It should be noted that the Select Committee did not ask us (the author was a member of both inquiries) to find out whether there was underachievement, but why.

However, in addition to its brief, Rampton was also able to confirm the problem of underachievement – and as was to be expected the Swann Report similarly confirmed this on a large scale when it appeared in March 1985. Dr Driver's report appeared to contradict previous findings on the question of underachievement. His study of five schools revealed that black pupils did better academically than did their white peers, especially the black girls. However, Driver, himself admitted the following in his report: 'This group is not meant to be a representative sample upon which nationwide predictions can be made' (Driver, 1980, p.9). He admitted that he was only able to go into those schools which would co-operate; at times, the relevant records were either missing or non-existent; and the social background of the pupils was outside his terms of reference.

But the admission which, for me as an educationist, puts to rest Driver's findings was that he did not take account of the effect of organizational, curricular and staffing situations within the five schools whose pupils were the concerns of his study. These are the key issues with which one must come to terms before one can have anything useful to say about academic achievement since they are the most important aspects of both the planned and the hidden curriculum. Additionally, it must be pointed out that Driver used no control group, and what is more, his sample was not random in selection. Driver's report might, therefore, be dismissed in preference for the numerous other findings of underachievement.

Professor Rutter, on the other hand, from various pieces of research addressed the Swann Committee on 'Growing Up in Inner London: Problems and Accomplishments'. His evidence also pointed to black pupils doing well. However, it was observed that black pupils needed to stay on in the sixth form longer than their indigenous peers.

One might reasonably infer that either there are additional obstacles for black pupils in the system or that they are naturally inferior. But the Jensen/Eysenck positions have been variously discredited (including by Swann) since they first appeared.

That we mislead our indigenous white pupils. there can be no doubt. Evidence of this, surely, might be gleaned from the activities of the National Front. Of course it is known that the real forces behind the National Front emanate from supposedly responsible people, but the degrading and insulting, racist and provocative behaviours are mostly carried out by youngsters many of whom are still at school. Their slogans and actions are clearly based upon misinformation about their ethnic peers.

In one study carried out on behalf of the Rampton Inquiry the researcher went to an all-white secondary school in a rural area. The following are just a few of many quotes taken from 13– and 14-year-olds who admitted that they had never met a black person but that they nevertheless had opinions about them:

> People from the West Indies mainly stay by themselves and don't mix with other people. Most West Indians live around the big cities like Coventry, Birmingham and Wolverhampton. Very few people live in the country. Back in the West Indies they live in shanty towns and eat coconuts all day.

> People from Africa are also black but you do not get many of them emigrating. In their country most of them live in the bush.

> A lot of the time immigrants complain about the way they are treated, the government, money, poor living conditions, etc. If all they can do is complain they shouldn't have come. It was their choice.

> I have learnt that a lot of the crime rate is due to the excess immigrants in the country. The immigrants who are mostly unemployed go around in gangs and commit violent crimes.

> I have learnt that they are pulling this country down because they all depend on social security.

These youngsters later become teachers who then go on to perpetuate the kind of myths, preconceptions and stereotypes reflected in the quotations given. Teachers very often expressed the views that black pupils are only excellent at sports and dancing but nothing else; that 'they all want to be brain surgeons' in reference to Asian pupils; that black pupils are anti-social, mischievous and loud; and that Asian pupils are quiet and well-behaved, and similar misinformed and dangerous views.

The real difficulty is that unlike 13-year-olds, teachers are in a position to effect actions based upon such views. Bernard Coard, it will be recalled, was spurred into writing his book *How the West Indian Child is Made Educationally Sub-normal in the British School System* by the fact of black pupils' over-representation in ESN schools. There is also considerable evidence to show that black pupils are more likely to find themselves in remedial streams, CSE as opposed to GCE groups, disruptive units than their indigenous counterparts. Similarly, they tend to suffer exclusions and suspensions at a higher rate. Since teachers are still largely responsible for devising the curriculum in schools, it follows that they are hardly likely to draw up schemes which will stretch their black pupils to become brain surgeons, for they start with doubts in relation to this possibility.

The Rampton/Swann Inquiry often met the reply that: 'we do not know how many ethnic minorities are in this school since we do not bother to notice colour. We treat all children alike.' Yet within minutes of this declaration by one headmaster he was to say that 'the trouble with West Indians is that they have a ghetto-like mentality'. When pressed for an explanation, he swivelled his chair to face and view from a window in his office which overlooked the school playground. Sure enough, he was able to illustrate his meaning by pointing to two groups of West Indian boys in the playground. 'That is what I mean', he declared. 'They are always together.' We couldn't help noticing that there were three groups of white boys together too. It is significant that the head appeared to be colour-blind; that he treated all children alike. Starting where pupils are, is the best way to motivate youngsters. And motivation is the next-door neighbour of achievement, however we define it.

To treat all pupils alike must necessarily fall short of this principle. The significant pointers to where the pupils are will necessarily be their cultural, religious, racial and linguistic backgrounds. Ignore this and we leave them behind. The Eurocentric educational pork will not be a palatable menu for all. Some will starve. In this respect, nothing is more inequitable than the well-meant but misguided adoption of the equal treatment for all principle. Pupils are not alike. So much for the question of 'why multicultural education'.

Our next question concerns identifying those factors within the educational system which then lead to underachievement for some and misinformation for others. Several factors contribute to this state of affairs: racism; poor (or no) pre-school provision; inadequate reading and language programmes; the curriculum; biased books and teaching materials; examination constraints; poor (or no) school pastoral arrangements; absence of links between the school and the community; disciplinary measures and special techniques; and career guidance as given. Racism and the curriculum will be examined in detail.

Racism

Racism describes a set of attitudes and behaviours towards people of another race which is based on the belief that races are distinct and can be graded as 'superior' or 'inferior'. A racist is, therefore, someone who believes that people of a particular race, colour or ethnic origin are inherently inferior, so that their identity, culture, self-esteem and views and feelings are of less value than his/her own, and can be disregarded or treated as less important.

This could be either overtly expressed or unintentionally displayed. The end-result is equally damaging to the recipient. The headmaster who treats all his pupils alike, the teacher who sees black pupils as only good sportsmen or women aspiring too highly, and the like, may be well-meaning in intention. The outcome is one of inferior provision for ethnic minorities. This is also a problem of institution.

Then there is institutionalized racism. Take, for example, a typical instrument of government for a secondary school. Nowhere in them will there be an overt expression of racism directed towards ethnic minorities. Yet to put into effect its categories of membership is almost certainly to exclude ethnic minorities. The requirements that local politicians should be in the majority; that there should be academic (university/professor?) representation or an industrialist are effectively closing avenues to ethnic minorities since these are areas which for similar reasons are largely closed to them. School governors are important people. They are responsible for all the senior appointments who, in turn, determine what happens in the school.

It is significant that so many government reports (Fifth Report from the House of Commons Home Affairs Committee, the Rampton Interim Report, the Scarman Report, and the Thompson Report), all appearing between June 1981 and October 1982, identified racism as at least one major hindrance to equal opportunities for ethnic minorities. The Swann Report echoes this rather loudly too.

The Curriculum (Planned and Hidden)

> Perhaps she could finish her father's unfinished work. He had been interested in savages and backward races. Africa was the best place to find such people, ... Mary would go to Africa. She could go among the wildest savages she could find. She would spend her life studying cannibals. (Red Book 1, 1968)

As teachers, we have the duty and responsibility to be selective and sensitive in our choice of materials for the consumption of young children who are in our care. Presenting the above to any class, let alone a multiracial one, would suggest recklessness at least in the execution of this duty. Yet this is only one of the examples which we found prevalent as we gathered evidence for our enquiry. Consider what message was being given to the indigenous white pupils of that classroom. Then consider what message was being received by the black pupils.

In view of this it is not surprising to see in the *Education Guardian* (2 May 1973) that a black child needed permission to represent himself in one of his own drawings. 'In a first-year art class at a South London Secondary School the topic was a local street scene. Studying the work of a West Indian girl the art teacher asked: "Why don't you draw any black people in the picture?"

'"Miss, are we allowed to?" came the reply.' This same negative view of one's self was reflected in the black girl's utterance after studying herself in a mirror: 'Ugh, aren't I black?'

The issues arising out of *Red Book 1* are not confined to the primary sector in education. Hugh Trevor-Roper's *The Rise of Christian Europe* will illustrate: 'Perhaps in the future there will be some African History to teach. But at present there is none, or very little; there is only the history of Europeans in Africa. The rest is largely darkness... and darkness is not a subject for history.'

Similar sentiments to those expressed in Trevor-Roper's work are currently to be found in standard works of reference which are in use in school today:

> To the conquest of nature through knowledge the contribution made by Asiatics has been negligible and by Africans (Egyptians excluded) non-existent. The printing-press and the telescope, the steam engine, the internal combustion engine and the aeroplane, the telegraph and telephone, wireless broadcasting and the cinematograph, the gramophone and television, together with all the leading discoveries in physiology, the circulation of the blood, the laws of respiration and the like, are the result of researches carried out by white men of European stock. (Fisher, 1945)

These references can have a damaging effect on ethnic minority children quite apart from presenting an inaccurate picture of the world to all children.

We still teach the different subject areas with a Eurocentric eye. Wilberforce and Lincoln we tell our pupils for example, single handedly brought about the emancipation of slavery. At least, this is what our children – black and white – understand. No mention is made of the work of black politicians some of whom sacrificed their lives to that end. Telemarque (Denmark) Vassey, Nat Turner, Nanny and the Maroons, Harriet Tubman, Sojourner Truth, Frederick Douglas, James Forten and others are either unheard of or deliberately forgotten. Yet their supreme contribution was necessarily greater than that of Wilberforce and Lincoln.

A simple test for anyone to carry out would be this: stop any ten school children and query who was Florence Nightingale. Ten out of ten will answer correctly. Our history books, hospital wards and £10 notes have ensured that Florence Nightingale's work is never forgotten. This is an excellent thing. Children do benefit in terms of motivation from having role-models around.

Mary Seacole's work is little known in schools. Mary Seacole, a born Jamaican, sold all her belongings and travelled to this country with a view to going with Florence Nightingale to the Crimea. The government would not sponsor her. Her colour was an obstacle. She used what little moneys she had left to travel there under her own steam. She set up in the more dangerous zones to achieve all that Florence Nightingale accomplished. True, she was honoured by a member of the Royal Family on her return, but silently forgotten thereafter. What equal worth she might be for black youngsters – what better image of black people she could convey to others!

Third World countries are often portrayed as recipients of aid in Geography textbooks and lessons. Rarely do we find anything mentioned of the fact that to a considerable extent Western civilization has been in the past, and is still today, dependent upon the fruits of the under-developed world. For example, Bristol and Cardiff are cities whose history should remind us most forcefully of this fact.

In a recent article David Wright criticized the racist and ethnocentric nature of two modern and popular geography text-books (1983). He concluded his critique thus:

> If teachers with sufficient expertise to be authors of standard textbooks write this insensitive material, what hope is there that other books and other lessons are less biased? At a conservative estimate 100,000 pupils have studied 'Man and his World'. Some of them are now policemen, teachers, social workers. Others will soon qualify in these fields. What will their attitudes to race be? (Wright, 1983, p.15)

Far too often Science and Mathematics teachers dismiss the multicultural curriculum as a worthy goal, but not applicable to their subject areas. These areas are regarded as culture-free and neutral in their presentation. In fact, nothing is further from the truth. These areas have as much contribution to make in altering the prejudiced and stereotyped preconceptions held of ethnic minorities as any other subject areas. Every subject taught in schools has a vital contribution to make.

It is difficult to understand why in a Biology lesson being given to nearly all black pupils the teacher insists on illustrating all points with 'blue eyes', 'pink skin', 'blue veins' and 'blond hair'. Close attention to the language and illustrations used in science lessons will soon put paid to the idea of neutrality. Science teachers wishing to come to terms with the multiracial society in which all pupils are growing up must seek to up-date the view given of the technology used in the application of science. All pupils must be helped to understand that science is an activity carried out by people everywhere and not solely a matter of research.

Science teachers will need to be much more selective about the types of textbooks and other teaching materials needed in order to avoid the stereotyping images of black people, sadly, still commonly portrayed. Science lessons could do much to explode some of the myths popularized about race, genetics and evolution theory. The need for science teachers to realize that science curricula are often culturally biased towards a European/North American view point, ignoring both the current and historical contributions of Africans, Indians, the Chinese and the Arabs, is a strong one. Not many of our pupils, for example, would learn at school that the first successful heart surgeon – Daniel Hale Williams – was a black man.

Ray Hemmings has demonstrated conclusively that the Chinese, the Egyptians, the Asians and others can be called upon to enrich the learning of Mathematics (1980). Consider, for example, Guru Nanak's birthday. At such times the Sikhs would decorate their walls, floors and elsewhere with beautiful geometric illustrations. Is this not a way to link such a vital study more closely with the cultural background of more of our pupils?

Historical mathematics is not an important end itself. But drawing upon it by way of illustrations at the appropriate times during mathematics lessons enables pupils to get a sounder perspective on the nature of mathematical activity. It could then be realized that this science has developed and is still developing out of the efforts of various societies to come to terms with some of the numerous problems with which they were faced and are facing. Extending the horizons of the traditional ethno-centric approach to Mathematics to include the contributions of different societies, such as their different counting systems, etc., has the following benefits:

  (a) ethnic minority children become more knowledgeable about their own cultural background. This way they are more likely to grant respect and meaning to their origins;
  (b) other children are allowed to share in the delights and richness of various other cultures;
  (c) the quality of Mathematical work will itself be enhanced by drawing upon such cultural diversity.

More truths via the curriculum and a few less lies. There is so much to tell this way. After all, the Hindu-Arabic numeral script is Hindi. The zero or cypher is a great invention because it is the origin of the denary system. With the zero, we can have the binary system, hence computers. Glass–amalgam is from the Middle East. Geometry and other mathematical sciences are from the Egyptians. The· magnetic compass – the magnetic needle – is from the Chinese. Saltpetre is from the Hindus, and it helped in exploding mines, e.g. coal, iron – note the Industrial Revolution.

My call, therefore, is for a balanced, more positive approach to the curriculum for all pupils – particularly in all-white schools. I reject Black Studies; I reject the Eurocentric curriculum. Children learn as much, if not more, via the hidden curriculum. How we staff our schools, how we organize our structures and the place we give to ethnic minority teachers in such structures will be important lessons for all our pupils. What kind of message is it that there should be so few black headteachers in the whole of this country? Are ethnic minorities in search of heroes?

A multicultural/anti-racist approach to the curriculum is required.

References

BOLTON, E.J. (1979). 'Education in a multiracial society', *Trends in Education* 4 (Winter).
COARD, B. (1971). *How the West Indian Child is made Educa-*

tionally Sub-normal in the British School System. Weston Favell: New Beacon.

COMMONWEALTH IMMIGRANTS ADVISORY COUNCIL (1964). Second Report. (Cmnd, 2266). London: HMSO.

DEPARTMENT OF EDUCATION AND SCIENCE (1965). *The Education of Immigrants*. Circular 7/65. London: DES.

DRIVER, G. (1980). *Beyond Under-Achievement*. Case Studies of English, West Indian and Asian School Leavers at 16+. London: Commission for Racial Equality.

FISHER, H.A.L. (1945 edn). *History of Europe*. London: Eyre and Spottiswoode.

HONEYFORD, R. (1984). 'Education and race – an alternative view', *Salisbury Review* 2, 2.

LITTLE, A. (1968). *The Education of Immigrant Pupils in Inner London Primary Schools*. London: ILEA.

NATIONAL ASSOCIATION FOR MULTICULTURAL EDUCATION (1980). 8, 3 (Summer); and 9, 1 (Autumn).

RAMPTON REPORT. GREAT BRITAIN. DEPARTMENT OF EDUCATION AND SCIENCE (1981). *West Indian Children in our Schools*, Cmnd 8723. London: HMSO.

RED BOOK 1. *An English Reader for Primary Children* (1968). 7th edn. London: Oliver and Boyd.

ROSE, E.J.B. (1969). *Colour and Citizenship*. London: Institute of Race Relations.

SELECT COMMITTEE OF THE HOUSE OF COMMONS (1977). HC 180, 1, 111.

SHARPE, G. (1764). The *Gentleman's Magazine*, 34, 493. In: FRYER, P. (1984) *Staying Power*. London: Pento Press, p.68.

STONE, M. (1981). *The Education of the Black Child in Britain*. London: Fontana.

SWANN REPORT. GREAT BRITAIN. DEPARTMENT OF EDUCATION AND SCIENCE (1985). *Committee of Inquiry into the Education of Children from Ethnic Minority Groups. Education for All*, Cmnd 9453. London: HMSO.

VERNON, P. (1965). *Environmental Handicaps and Intellectual Development*.

WEST INDIAN PUPILS IN REDBRIDGE (1978). *Cause for Concern*. Redbridge: Black People's Progressive Association/ Redbridge Community Relations Council.

WRIGHT, D. (1983). 'The geography of race', *Times Educational Supplement*, 15 July, 15. (Books criticized: DAWSON, J.A. and THOMAS, D. (1975) *Man and his World;* WHYNNE-HAMMOND, C. (1979) *Elements of Human Geography.*)

7   In-Service Strategies for Teacher Education

Wendy Robertson

The proliferation of post-Swann discussions has generated a good deal of rhetoric and recommendation about principles of good practice education in the light of received knowledge about the issue of race in modern Britain; ways in which the task of in-service education should be approached are relevant to this discussion.

The development of our work in multicultural and anti-racist education at Sunderland Polytechnic has one locus in the development of theoretical concepts signalled by other papers presented at this conference; the other locus is the established tradition within the faculty for curriculum development through active inquiry with its focus on teachers' professional development. This latter tradition as applied to the issue of multicultural and anti-racist education is the theme of this paper.

Discussions about strategy in education range along a continuum of optimism and pessimism, depending on the views of the role which education in all its facets may play in the development of greater justice and equality in British society. To what degree can educational processes be instrumental in this development? To what degree is it changes in perceptions and understandings of society which will provide the source of change? To what degree are changes in education impossible without a generating change in society itself?

In my work I am interested in the polarity which is placed around a notion of whether theories and theorizing generates good practice or whether good practice* bases itself *in action* around the

---

* The problem of defining 'good practice' is acknowledged.

emergent practical theorizing of teaching practitioners themselves.

So, on the one hand, there is the view that change in practice and approach will only ensue when the individual's understanding of fundamental issues has changed. In this view, alterations of fundamental understanding can only be generated from the students' abstract thinking and conceptualization. For instance, s/he has to understand and identify racism as a concept. S/he has to recognize the critical tension between the concept of multiculturalism and anti-racism. S/he has to be able to rehearse the relationship between race and culture and culture and power. It follows, in this view, that once the teacher-student internalizes the concepts and can argue the issues, the practice will change. Then, illuminated by this insight, her/his practice and operation in school is modified and enhanced along acceptable multicultural or anti-racist lines.

On the other hand, there is the view which is argued in this paper that changes in practice are more likely to emerge from the constraints of the practical situation. Having worked with teachers in the training and the in-service setting, across a range of experience, I would propose that change of practice tends to be reactive, pragmatic and intuitive. This process is not seen as *inferior* to the notion of change emerging from intellectual decision. It is a process which is qualitatively different, but which recognizes the way in which teachers operate under minute-by-minute pressure where instinct and feeling inform immediate action. Conceptualization and cognition may be bedded within that instinctive action; alternatively, it may require the practitioners to act *against* their instincts. Focus on action and practice is about recognizing and confronting these contradictory instincts as elements in a teacher's own normal procedures.

In recognition of this we try as teacher-educators in the initial and in-service field to give proper recognition to the fact that changes in practice may emerge from focused practical endeavours as much as cognitive activity. These practical endeavours, when identified, recorded as evidence, evaluated and systematically reflected upon should be the core of a teacher's learning processes. This kind of work, combined with inputs of information and ideas, leads teachers to reach a higher level of conceptualization of their own professional task, a higher degree of control of the educational process. Within such processes, the conceptual development of the teacher is located professionally and psychologically in the classroom and the school.

This notion of teacher development will not allow the teacher to separate the rhetoric of good anti-racist and multicultural education from the practice in the classroom and the school. Strategies which endorse this approach will not allow a teacher to protest 'that's all very well in theory, but you should see my school, full of bigoted parochial people'. The process and content development work will demand strategies to take this into account. Such courses will not allow the teacher to protest 'It's a good idea, but I don't have the skills to put it into practice', as within the course these skills will be developed. Students emerging from such courses will not protest 'It's all very well, but I have so much to do, so many priorities' because within the course they will have developed, in practice, the recognition that what is at issue is *fundamentally good education*, and in that sense they will be at the centre, not the periphery, of their main professional experience.

Efforts to transform these principles into practice in our work at pre-service and in-service levels have led to a general operational principle of permeation in all our courses. Each aspect of the major undergraduate and in-service teacher education courses has been considered for the degree to which it may meet multicultural and/or anti-racist principles. The degree to which this is/is not carried out in practice is naturally an important issue. There is evidence that a multicultural and anti-racist principle is there in terms of information input and as a criterion for professional self-appraisal. Students have assessed work which may reveal the principle in operation. However, there is still room for development in some aspects of the larger courses. In terms of broad strategy, thinking in the faculty about the professional location of in-service initiatives has been informed by the survey of ten schools in five authorities in the region (Adamson *et al.*, 1985). This was based on 40 interviews and an emergent questionnaire survey of 200 teachers, and was concerned with teacher approaches in areas of low ethnic minority settlements. We are about to use the survey instrument in an in-depth study in three local authorities, where 3200 teachers will be surveyed. This should aid the development of models of in-service learning which could be tailored to particular schools or particular settings. This stage in the survey has been consistently held up during the teacher action but we hope to complete it before the summer of 1987.

It would be useful at this point to consider the main findings of the survey and consider ways in which it can contribute to the planning of in-service work. Of course one is always cautious about taking on board an oversimplification of teachers' attitudes. However, illuminating information emerged which developed our understanding and allowed us to consider approaches to strategy. The 40 interviews and the final analysis which threw up six significant factors allowed us to flesh out our understanding of the range and complexity of teachers' attitudes and understandings in this field of education. The factors may be seen to fall into two groups, contextual and developmental. Individual teachers, departments and schools were factors in various configurations which could have implications for individual, departmental and LEA policies.

Contextual Factors

Complacency

Teachers showing this characteristic thought they already educated for tolerance and towards equality. Ethnic minority pupils that have been in their care have been accepted by the other children. For these teachers, the strategy of recognizing and drawing attention to prejudice was thought to increase the problem for the children. These teachers accepted that their subject was probably written up in a biased fashion. They resent condescensions which they see in some 'multicultural' materials, and can't see any need in their school for 'multicultural education'.

Action here would have to incorporate active inquiry which obliged the teachers, as individuals or in groups, to take to pieces their own taken-for-granted view. Questions about how and where the 'education for tolerance and equality' was *evident* in their practice would be appropriate. A whole category of information about the broad reality of British society and the interdependence across Britain and across the world would be needed.

Attribution of Racism to Pupils

The schools in the survey, which were mostly in areas of low ethnic minority settlement, contained teachers and groups of teachers who considered that there is inbuilt racism in their pupils. As well as this, they saw the pupils as characteristically being suspicious of outsiders – i.e. anyone outside their own community. This inbuilt racism, in their view, came from the parents' views about race. According to the teachers, the pupils' ideas about people from ethnic minority groups do not come from their own direct experience. They absorb general prejudice from their parents, e.g. regarding an alleged relationship between ethnic minority presence and unemployment.

Action here would involve the challenge regarding the 'received' racism of the pupils. Does putting the 'blame' on the parents absolve teachers from any responsibility for counter-action? Active inquiry into the roots of prejudice which lie in parochial attitudes would be productive for both the teachers and pupils. Evidence of discussions among staff regarding the extension of the curriculum to reduce parochialism and ethnocentrism could allow teachers to reflect on their own taken-for-granted views on the curriculum.

Professional Disengagement

Here some teachers acknowledged that they themselves have had no contact, and are without experience of a range of people from different minority groups. They had no knowledge, no information and do not see any necessity for multicultural education to have priority in their schools.

Strategies where this factor is strong could not assume any knowledge on the part of the teachers. The first task is to get them to listen, to participate at all. Schools where such a factor is strong can resist innovatory attempts even in an authority which has a policy and which is insisting on each school developing policies and action plans. Strategies with such schools should involve some sort of experience of collaborative exchange at a staff level. The exchange or collaboration needs to be with a school which is, perhaps, more evidently culturally diverse, where teachers are recognizing and acting on the extension of curriculum practices and opportunities which this offers.

Should these contextual factors consistently come together in one institution, then the possibility of making development through individual attendance at courses may be limited. Such a situation would invite whole-school in-service strategies and collaboration between schools. Such strategies have at their base a strong challenge to the teachers' own taken-for-granted assumptions about what constituted the 'reality' of the teaching situation in which they find themselves.

In such whole-school in-service work, one would need to incorporate a broad need for information, but this should also involve systematic inquiry to check out, to unpack teachers' global assumptions about both the children they teach and the professional situation in which they find themselves.

Any authority attempting to implement a policy may encounter schools and groups of teachers who emerge from such contexts. They may meet a blank self-justifying wall. In-service initiative needs to be critical and self-evaluating in tone, but carried out in a collaborative context where the teachers feel sufficiently confident to take risks, and to reflect systematically on their own practice.

Developmental Factors

A more optimistic environment would be characterized by the confluence of the three *developmental* factors.

1. Positive Innovative Attitude

These teachers showed concern about the possibilities of inbuilt racism. They saw British society as being enriched by being culturally diverse, and an education system which reflected this as necessary for their school and for the development of an equal society. Such teachers have positive approaches to combating prejudice. They looked forward to obtaining more resources and obtaining relevant information and were open to new developments in this area.

Such teachers, departments and schools appear to be ripe for broad development. One cannot, however, take for granted that such teachers will automatically take up resources and teach in a fashion which of itself is good multicultural or anti-racist education. Critical self-examination can show that teachers do not necessarily use new approaches and new material in an unprejudicial fashion.

2. Receptivity towards Practical Experience

Teachers scoring highly on this factor were interested in a whole range of experience to develop their knowledge and insight. They showed particular interest in exchange with schools in more culturally diverse areas.

Such openness is only of value in changing approaches if the LEAs support action by facilitating strategies of exchange.

3. Awareness of Importance of Materials

These people saw that materials could reinforce prejudice and were aware of the dangers of bias.

Appraisal and critique of materials is often a first stage in any multicultural or anti-racist strategy and of itself can be a consciousness-raising exercise. It can be a very short-term one unless it encompasses strategies for using material, which may be seen as racist, in a way which may reduce prejudice. It should also involve close self-analysis of a teacher's own use of materials and long-term strategies for materials development.

General Implications for Strategies Emerging from the Survey

The crystallization of these factors, illuminated by the in-depth data from the survey, leads to a range of general implications for broad strategies at authority and school levels which may be modified depending on the particular profile of a department, school or area. The need for fundamental change, rather than token gestures, was always evident. An increasing certainty emerged that there was a need for organic developments within the schools which would challenge the taken-for-granted assumptions. These developments would extend the teacher's accepted criteria for judging the work and the operation of a school and develop new strategies for action appropriate to particular professional contexts.

Given the position proposed earlier that a teacher's practice is changed by heightening the teacher's self-awareness in the professional context, strategies which would be appropriate in the light of these factors suggest themselves.

1. *The building up of evidence* (e.g. audio/video tapes, transcripts, fieldnotes, children's work products). Such records of actual classroom action could be appraised by the interested teacher group. Group analysis would reveal teachers' expectations about pupils, assumptions about what counts as pupil progress, what counts as appropriate curriculum content and a legitimate view of British society.

2. *Structured co-operative inquiry* into teachers' own normal teaching process content and materials, using actual evidence which may be shared within the co-operative group. Deep-seated attitudes and values would have to be encountered and dealt with within this inquiry. It is appropriate, given our other evidence, that teachers should become aware of their own value positions in relation to those of their colleagues. Such co-operative inquiry eventually and ideally could involve comparison of teaching content and processes across subject areas and across departments – even across schools – and would lead to new patterns of practice.

3. *Inter-school networks*, which could involve exchange of teachers, children and material. These networks could involve the rural – urban continuum, as well as the monocultural – multicultural continuum, to extend both pupils and teachers out of parochial contexts. Using guiding principles about education in a culturally diverse society as a focus, the teachers may then develop new ways of seeing their own work in relation to that of others, and establish new common traditions of practice in a region.

These insights have informed course development in Sunderland Polytechnic's Faculty of Education, and underpin thinking in the pattern of in-service course development. It has involved the development of an In-Service Certificate, an M.Ed. in Multicultural Education and a proposal for a 25-day full-time DES course in Education for Cultural Diversity in addition to providing new criteria for judging existing courses.

One important element in all these course initiatives is the demand for in-depth and documented appraisal and analysis of the actual learning and school situations. These bring about changes in the general approaches to education involving new criteria for judgement of good practice. Because of the changes in the actual practice in the classrooms and schools, the potential of these students to influence their colleagues by their action can be enhanced. The teachers involved can argue and negotiate using evidence from the practical situation which appeals to other practitioners. They have an increasingly sensitive vocabulary with which to articulate the increasingly complex practical factors which are emerging. They can use the clarion call of 'good education' and substantively justify it.

Naturally our teacher-students will, as a general part of their course, encounter and discuss fundamental concepts and issues emerging from theories of multicultural and anti-racist education, They hear leading speakers in the field, and may locate their own 'practical theorizing' in the light of these broader concepts.

However, it is argued here that without a *rigorous practical element* there is the danger of the teacher-student separating such theory from the constraints of practice. Without this element, they may be able to answer perfect examination questions and they may write wonderful dissertations, but their practice *will remain the same*. Such an outcome belies the fundamental purpose of all in-service teacher education.

References

ADAMSON, G.F., BIOTT, C., LYNCH, J. and ROBERTSON, W. (1985). Beyond the policy threshold: living with dilemmas and negotiating principles for action'. In: CARTER, A. (Ed) *Teachers for Multicultural Society*. London : Longman/Schools Council.

BIOTT, C. and LYNCH. J. (1983). Towards the Multicultural Curriculum: Evaluation. Durham ATO Regional Committee.

BIOTT, C., LYNCH, J. and ROBERTSON, W. (1984). 'Supporting teachers' own progress towards multicultural education', *Multicultural Teaching*, II, 2 (Spring), 30 – 41.

8 An Outline of Multicultural Education Development in an Area of north-east England

Patricia Keel

The north-east region of Britain has been viewed by both outsiders and many of those inside the region as being one generally untouched by the settlement of ethnic minorities. Indeed, the term 'all-white' can justifiably be used to refer to many schools and whole geographical areas. Hence the frequent evidence of teachers taking the view that 'we don't have that problem here' (Biott, Robertson and Lynch, 1983).

With a national average of 'black'[1] population reckoned at 3–4 per cent the average for the whole of the north-east is probably considerably lower, given that Newcastle upon Tyne and Middlesborough have the largest settlements of around 3–4 per cent and all other areas much lower percentages. Within Newcastle itself, there is a concentration of settlement from the New Commonwealth in the West End of the city, the highest percentage of 11 per cent in Wingrove (1981 Census) (Actual figures could have altered in recent years.) In the following account, focus will fall on the five authorities of Tyne and Wear, and on Newcastle upon Tyne in particular, rather than on the north east as a whole.

It may be worth noting that within Tyne and Wear there is a long-established Jewish community with a strong cultural identity. Gateshead is the site of the Talmudical College, a religious and cultural centre of world renown. The Jewish community in the region offers a pattern of development worth considering in discussion of issues such as religious and cultural separatism, as against assimilation and so-called integration. Here is a community many of whom maintain a way of life in several aspects parallel to that, say, of Muslims. They have, since the early part of this century successfully preserved their distinct character – their separate schools, shops, holidays, particular mode of dress, etc. – all generally accepted by the larger community and supported by the authorities. But long before the Jews settled, the region became the home of a large number of Catholics who also sustain their religious identity in their churches and separate schools. Perhaps more remarkable is the presence for over 100 years of an Arab community in South Shields. They originated from groups of seamen who were grounded there while working on British ships (Carey, 1984). Another example of prolonged contact with non-Europeans was recently (June 1985) highlighted at a seminar, 'Contemporary Japan', organized by the Japanese Embassy at Sunderland Polytechnic to mark the opening of the Nissan car factory in Washington. Few people are now aware of the presence of the Japanese in the region during the early part of this century when several of the outstanding ships in their navy were built here. Records show the fraternization and cultural exchange which took place during those years.

Insularity

However, these local contacts with people of other backgrounds appear by and large to have gone unnoticed. As a librarian there said: 'one of the problems is that you can live in the region all your life and never know there are black people around.' Among the general public the tone seems to be one of comparative insularity. 'Outsiders', be they black or white, often vouch for this. Some football fans have shown a high level of racist behaviour, and it is known that the National Front find their recruiting efforts worthwhile and they succeed in making their presence felt. Moreover, the survey of teachers' attitudes in the region carried out by Sunderland Polytechnic (Biott, Robertson and Lynch, 1983) revealed a range of responses, many of which could be seen as negative towards the notion of educating for a multicultural society. For example, 40 per cent of those surveyed thought that attention to multicultural education was not necessary in their school. Attitudes have probably shifted to some extent at least since this survey was made. A further survey is being planned by

Sunderland Polytechnic with the co-operation of the Newcastle Education Advisory Service.

Response in Education

The earliest response to the presence of non-white ethnic minority children in schools was to arrange for provision of English as a second language (E2L). Manor Park in Newcastle upon Tyne was, nearly a decade ago, the first of several E2L centres set up in the region. Children have been sent to these centres, often housed with remedial units, for varying lengths of time to be immersed primarily in English until they are thought able to cope in their classrooms at school. Teachers have thus been able initially to lay the burden of 'a child with a language problem' at the door of those centres. In the light of current feeling about such centres, reinforced in the Swann Report (1985), there are moves being made now, especially in Newcastle, to modify this practice. It is intended to employ several peripatetic bilingual teachers, who will be responsible in schools for the bilingual development of ethnic minority children.[2] This move implies a fresh approach to the question of 'mother-tongue' provision, which has been debated in Newcastle over the past couple of years. The authority has been providing £10,000 a year to support mother tongue classes run by the communities themselves. The newer approach to language has been prompted by staff at Westgate Hill Infants where some 80 per cent of children are bilingual. The headteacher (now appointed teacher-adviser for multicultural education) talks frequently about 'the waste of throwing out all this bilingualism'. Thus there is an awareness of the language issues, but virtually no new action as yet. With Swann declaring that schools are not to be expected to provide community languages, it seems unlikely that original intentions will be acted upon.

Growing alongside the original concern for English language provision, contact between individual teachers in schools or members of the advisory services and religious and/or community leaders led at first to what has been termed 'compensatory education'. As one adviser put it:

. . . in line with national and government thinking, in fact multicultural education was for quite a long time compensatory education. It would be initially E2L followed fairly closely by looking at the dietary needs of the children, their difficulties in wearing certain clothes and any hostility that was being shown towards them in schools and the endeavours of all five LEAs probably were aimed initially at providing these things, or catering for ethnic minority children, without an awareness that it mattered in schools where there were no black children.

However, an interest has developed, particularly more recently, in a growing number of schools in the area, in certain aspects of multicultural education. Festival-celebrating, for instance, has become popular in many primary schools, while a 'world studies' approach to introducing other countries is favoured by some teachers at upper junior and secondary level. Elements like these are fitted in and around the 'usual' curriculum. Whereas most schools have little or no ethnic minority presence, there are a handful, again in Newcastle. where there are significant numbers on-roll. Westgate Hill Infants is estimated to have nearly 80 per cent, the highest among a group of schools in the city's West End. Some of these schools, especially Westgate Hill Infants, have been influential in spreading multicultural education philosophy and are referred to as examples where good practice takes place. Others with fewer ethnic minority children, like Westerhope First, could also be cited. There are several individual teachers and advisers in the city who play an active part in promoting what is still popularly referred to as multicultural education, but one of them has said: 'We've got a long way to go in helping teachers to understand what racism is all about, institutional racism, personal racism, discrimination, what are the differences, and what teachers can do about it'. This remark pinpoints the crux of the matter: how is thinking to be moved along, so that the essential element of anti-racism within multicultural education is generally appreciated and acted upon?

Scarman Brings Change

A catalyst for such a movement in thinking came with the Scarman Report in 1981. Councils were called upon to set up procedures for monitoring racial equality as required by the 1976 Race Relations

Act. In Newcastle upon Tyne a wide-ranging response began. A Racial Equality Sub-Committee was established in 1982. It asked every department in the authority to state its policy and practice in writing. From the replies a consultative document emerged and this was circulated back to every department and further responses requested.

The Education Department had already set up the Racial Harmony Working Party in partnership with the Tyne and Wear Community Relations Council (CRC) whose role has been considerable in bringing pressure for change in the region. The group produced a report defining multicultural education, citing those schools where it was in practice and making several recommendations. This document went towards the shaping of the Education Committee's policy document on multicultural education.

The Racial Equality Consultation Document had several responses, notably that from the newly formed Newcastle branch of the then National Association for Multiracial Education (NAME). They were instrumental in several amendments being made which emphasized a more anti-racist stance. The group has been active in promoting anti-racist/multicultural philosophy, organizing public events and working systematically on tasks such as identifying anti-racist resources for education and examining materials for racial bias. Racism awareness courses were run by the group at a time when racism awareness training (RAT) was still generally disapproved in the region. Large numbers of people were not attracted, and the membership of the group remains a core of the 'converted'. However, this core has consisted of people who are influential in the city. That influence is evident in the distinct flavour of the city's policy, which focuses on racism as a root-problem. The group has helped to keep the city's policy on course in a field where main issues can easily become lost. Their recent seminar on the Swann Report was a good example of this. The keynote speakers of considerable experience informed on the political and social background to the Report and the implications for future developments.

Further debate on the consultative document was facilitated by the CRC at a conference early in 1984. What emerged was the CRC's policy statement on racial equality and an action plan (City of Newcastle, 1984). From the outset this document identifies racism as the main target for attack, and the theme of equality of access to all services in the city flows throughout. A seminar was held in October 1985 to review the action plan. Every department, including education, reported to the chief executive – who is backed by a policy services department – on progress made and on areas for further action. The other authorities in the region do not appear to have a process of consultation and documentation as energetic and pervasive as that in Newcastle, yet in the long run may have made as much progress. Obviously the combination of factors – the presence of pressure groups, policy-makers with an awareness of racial issues, individuals and particularly elected members prepared to take initiative in this field – have been different in each case. In one authority it was largely through the initiative of one adviser that a policy did appear. Newcastle upon Tyne tends to lead especially in liberal directions. Other authorities appear to have followed in this particular case, 'catching up' when they all put out policy statements on equality of access in education. The background to their appearance is traced below.

Education Policy Documents

Harking back chronologically to 1983, another significant catalyst for action which affected all five LEAs was a conference 'Education for Racial Harmony', organized at Otterburn by the Commission for Racial Equality (CRE) and Tyne and Wear's CRC. Gathered together were directors of education, deputy directors, education committee chairpersons, advisers, headteachers and school governors to be addressed by Gerry German (CRE), Carlton Duncan (Swann Committee), Trevor Carter and Gillian Klein (ILEA) on issues surrounding multicultural education. Certainly, interest and controversy were aroused, and reactions were varied. The five LEAs were urged to produce policies on multicultural education. Working parties have been set up and during the past couple of years policies from all five authorities have appeared. They are different in emphasis and a brief analysis of them may be worthwhile here.

   The documents from Sunderland, South Tyneside, North Tyneside and Gateshead all begin from the basis of the law as stated in section 71 of the Race Relations Act 1976, each declaring a policy of providing equality of opportunity in education in accordance with this law. North Tyneside went on to state:

> . . . that the content and scope of the curriculum and the nature of teaching materials shall reflect the multicultural nature of both British society and the world.
> That the ethos of each educational institution shall foster attitudes, relationships and habits through which may develop a respect and understanding of others of whatever national, racial, religious or cultural origin.

This document makes no further elaboration as do the others. However, South Tyneside adds to the substance of the above with the following:

> The importance of ensuring that children from ethnic minority groups have access to an education service relevant to their needs and which will enable them to play their full part as equals in society.

This document goes further in discussing implementation. Proposed action centres around ethnic minority children's needs. Schools are to be informed about 'matters of culture, dress, diet' and to be provided with 'a calendar of days of cultural observance as a source of information and as a teaching aid'. There is to be E2L provision, and ethnic minority parents are to be informed about education provision and their rights and responsibilities. There is to be 'a collection and maintenance of up-to-date statistics relating to the recognised needs of ethnic minority groups within the education system'. Also proposed is 'in-service courses for teachers on all aspects of multicultural education'. To support the efforts, it is stated that section 11 and EEC funding will be applied for. Also stated is the intention to monitor 'the overall effectiveness of the policy and to report to the Education Committee annually'.

The Sunderland and Gateshead policies are similar, especially in the emphasis placed on ethnic minority needs. However, these two do mention 'mother tongue'. Sunderland states that the authority has a responsibility to meet the needs of minority ethnic groups by 'providing facilities' for mother tongue teaching and the maintenance of cultural identity. Gateshead states that a register of ethnic minority pupils will allow adequate planning for E2L and for 'the support (if necessary) for mother tongue teaching'.

The major difference seen in the Newcastle document is the way it is prefaced by the CRC's policy statement on racial equality. This focuses squarely on racism and the need to counter it in promoting racial justice. The statement begins unequivocally: 'Racism exists in Newcastle. It creates disadvantages, discrimination and fear.' Focus is maintained on racism as the central issue, rather than on the issues of 'needs', 'provision' and 'spending', related to the presence of ethnic minorities:

> Specific spending proposals to overcome specific needs are important. But the achievement of the Racial Equality objectives will take much more effort than the simple expenditure of money. The main concern is with attitudes, and attitudes can be changed only over a period of time by persuasion and example, teaching and training. It is that above all which will require the Council's continued commitment.

It is a matter for debate whether this approach is likely to be more effective in bringing about change in the desired directions, assuming the directions desired are in fact the same for all parties. Those at the receiving end of racial injustice will probably say that it is essential to focus on racism as the root-cause of this injustice, but that the allocation of resources for positive action is equally essential.

Policies in Action

How have these five policies for education worked in action? Producing the policy documents generated a lot of work, especially in Newcastle upon Tyne. So far, however, there seems more paperwork than action for change: responses to policy statements, followed by more drafting of policies by each school or institution, and calls for more meetings, minutes and reports. For example, some authorities required written responses to the policy document from every school. It is reported how a number of schools were thrown into some confusion over producing what might be seen to be an appropriate response. (The paper here by Mould discusses this in greater detail.) There were some statements like: 'we treat all children alike', and 'we have no multicultural area near this school' and 'this really does not concern us here'. Nevertheless, this exercise was probably valuable in obliging all schools to become aware of the issue. As an adviser said: 'Every school has had to produce a document. Now that could be tokenism, it could be lipservice, but at least everyone has had to start thinking about it.'

All the five authorities have now either designated responsibility for multicultural education to an adviser already in post or appointed a local teacher adviser for this work. North Tyneside applied for and received substantial funding for a multicultural education centre. Several section 11 teachers have been appointed; a very small number are of ethnic minority background. The precise duties of these teachers has not been clear, and the confusion arises out of the root-dilemmas posed by section 11 regulations, not least its tendency to perpetuate a 'them and us' dichotomy. With their odd status and rather vaguely defined duties, these teachers, particularly if they are from ethnic minorities, have difficulty fitting in with the regular staff, who may have totally unrealistic expectations of them (Samran, 1986). In Newcastle, section 11 teachers hope that a new support network with the teacher adviser in charge will help sort out these difficulties. The ethnic minority teachers in these posts have proved the great advantage of having teachers who can communicate with parents in their own languages. It seems that a way needs to be cleared by which suitable people can be recruited to carry out vital school – parent liaison while they are in the process of acquiring qualified teacher status.

Those whose role is advisory hold at present a large responsibility in shaping policy and practice in the region. In order to achieve any significant change, it seems imperative that they should have a developed awareness of racial issues on a wide scale, and a commitment to lobbying for a black share in policy-making and the resulting action. The contribution black people are waiting to make in society needs to be recognized, welcomed and valued. Usual criteria, often based on stereotypical notions about qualifications, experience and suitability for jobs, need reassessing if black people are to take their place in the decision-making process.

In-service Training

Both Newcastle upon Tyne and North Tyneside Education Authorities have initiated in-service training programmes. Newcastle began in October 1983 with an awareness course for headteachers. This was followed the next year with a similar course for a representative teacher from every school. One of the organizers said:

> We were concerned that it wasn't just teachers from schools which had ethnic minority children there, but an issue for all children in all schools. In fact our objectives were to make clear that it wasn't a multicultural subject, it was something that was pervasive of the whole curriculum. It was quite successful and generated a lot of interest, but then because of the industrial action, we didn't follow that up as quickly as I think we ought to have done.

Indeed, the prolonged teachers' dispute probably considerably slowed the progress that otherwise may have been made.

Within the north-east region, the Education Faculty at Sunderland Polytechnic has taken a lead in the field of multicultural education. The department was involved in the evaluation of a regional DES course 'Towards a Multicultural Curriculum'. It was engaged also in an inquiry, with the then Schools Council funding, in ten schools in five LEAs, aimed at constructing propositions about in-service provision and other forms of support needed by teachers in order to implement multicultural anti-racist education (Adamson *et al.*, 1985). The nationally co-ordinated course 'Training the Trainers' attended by LEA advisers, teacher educators and senior staff from schools in the north-east has had influence in moving policy and practice within the region.

The department now runs their Certificate in Education for a Multicultural Society at the Education Development Centre in Newcastle, where much interest has been generated despite the current teachers' dispute. The course seeks to develop critical discourse regarding the issue of professional practice in the field of anti-racist/multicultural education. Members on the course are encouraged to use their own classroom work to raise evidence which can be analysed in order to enhance professional awareness, particularly in their handling of race-related topics. One of the later assignments is developing teaching materials suitable for this kind of education. The course thus bases discussion of fundamental issues in the fields of race and education within the context of classroom practice. An M.Ed. in Multicultural Education began in Autumn 1986. This is intended to have a similar action-based approach.

Resources

While a change in attitudes is at the heart of the process towards implementing anti-racist/multicultural education, the role played by resources cannot be underestimated. Over the past five years there has been a proliferation of materials for use in the field. Not all of it has been good, as a librarian has said, 'There's been a whole range of tokenistic materials produced as publishers cottoned on to the bandwagon'. But it has been helpful when teachers could be presented with appropriate material. Newcastle upon Tyne has been fortunate in an extremely supportive librarian who manages the authority's extensive education library service. A substantial allocation of resources has helped build an excellent stock of books and other materials, housed attractively at the Education Development Centre. A systematic programme was run in 1985-86 which included a course in awareness of the multi-ethnic society for the city's librarians. There is a touring exhibition for schools which the librarian introduces with an incisive 20-minute talk to teachers, putting across the main issues in anti-racist/multicultural education, approached via a critical examination of books and materials. Reactions from teachers to these issues can be mixed, as she explains:

> I refer to them and leave the resources in the school so that the issues are discussed. Sometimes I get a very hard time in schools. Sometimes there's a sympathetic response, but once I've actually been in a school then it seems to have an impact and creates a demand. Just today there was a teacher who was in one school where they were very active and he's gone to another school where there was nothing going on. So the word is spreading. We've got a tremendously long way to go. Schools

are only just beginning to understand multiculturalism and yet in a national sense they're moving much more towards an anti-racist approach. I would like to see an anti-racist approach adopted.

Anti-Racist Approach

Indeed, an anti-racist approach is being adopted increasingly by most of those in the front line in the area, as is the case nationally. It is interesting to trace how the consternation with which Chris Mullard's address at NAME's National Conference in 1984 was greeted has since dissolved. Now his call for the emphasis on anti-racist teaching in that exhortation is much more widely recognized, although there remains a general squeamishness over his particular ideological approach. Teachers have been traditionally encouraged to keep a safe distance between their work and politics, and many of them have been inclined to link multicultural education, and later anti-racist education, with politics on the left. Now given the authorities' present policies, increasing numbers (but still probably a minority) seem willing to take on multicultural education as a good cause, especially if it can be sold to them as 'good education', safe from any politics. However, in their recent analysis of the evolution of discourse in the field from an assimilationist stance, followed by the integrationist/multicultural through to the current anti-racist one, Troyna and Williams (1986) suggest that although an acknowledgement of racism as a core consideration has at last appeared, at least in some LEAs, nevertheless this movement can remain sterile if racism is not set in the overall context of disadvantage and inequality in our society. For an understanding of how racism operates, its process must be seen in relation to society's other processes, since it is not an isolated phenomenon.

Current anti-racism is tending to treat racism as a temporary illness or affliction that can be cured, as Shah (1986) says, 'like a boil on your back', by racism awareness training (RAT). A rolling programme of RAT has begun in Newcastle upon Tyne for everyone in the education service. The Industrial Language Training Unit also provides 'help in implementing equal opportunities' to a range of clientele, including some in the private sector. Nationally there is no evidence that RAT has positive results. Indeed, there is a danger of negative attitudes becoming entrenched, especially if those administering courses are not fully equipped to counter every kind of racist thinking. Moreover, using unprepared black people to speak about 'the black experience' can prove bewildering and hurtful for them. Their contribution could reinforce prejudice. The RAT programmes need strategies carefully worked out by experienced white and black trainers, working as a team. Arranging for independent evaluation of courses and their impact would help credibility.

The concern over race has been looked upon by a number of people as a 'bandwagon' that will eventually go away. However, time, interest and even resources, continue to come its way. All manner of bedfellows have come together, while others have been put apart in its cause. The CRC has sponsored, over the past few years, a working party drawn from the five LEAs to work on multicultural education guidelines for teachers in the region. A book is now available (Newcastle upon Tyne CRC, 1986) and has useful information for teachers, especially in respect of resources in the north-east. A tri-annual newsletter, *North East Multi-Racial Education*, is published by the head of Cleveland's Centre for Multicultural Education in Middlesborough. It informs on a variety of regional news and activities and carries useful feature articles. More recently, regional representatives to a national seminar of the Anti-Racist Teacher Network (ARTEN) were asked to form a north-east section. The group, representing teacher training and further education institutions, education advisers, teachers and members of the CRC, have shown interest in encouraging teacher training institutions to assess such areas as course content and development, recruitment of staff and students and staff development, particularly in relation to documents on these subjects put out by the DES, the Council for National Academic Awards and Council for Accreditation of Teacher Education. A working seminar in May 1986 drew a reasonable representation of policy-makers from local authorities, education institutions and ethnic minority communities to exchange ideas (Sisterson and Moore, 1986).

The Ethnic Minority Communities

Meanwhile there are the ethnic minority communities themselves, surrounded by, but generally remote from, all the talk and paperwork. It has been said both by members of the ethnic minority communities and a few people working in the field that there is a lack of contact with and involvement by the communities themselves. In recent articles Ng, Qureshi and Walker have expressed the vulnerability of local ethnic minority communities in their dependence on authorities to take into account their particular backgrounds and needs. Representation is mainly in the hands of a few CRC staff who have been expected to oversee a wide range of interests and feelings of several very different communities. The CRC staff themselves tend to take their guidance from the proclaimed leaders of communities, but do the leaders' views and perspectives always coincide with those of the rest of their community? As one education adviser put it, there is a need 'to get closer to people in ethnic minority communities, get to know them and establish a dialogue with them'. The initiative must come from the general community for this, but this is not always recognized. Nor is it recognized that mere dialogue or consultation will not be sufficient – ethnic minorities must take part in decision-making processes if equality is a genuine policy. Several new posts have been created during the past few years for work in various departments requiring the use of community languages. They are funded by section 11 and more particularly by the Manpower Services Commission. Most of the posts are, therefore, not permanent and their holders cannot help looking warily over their shoulders for their likely successors. Such an atmosphere does not generate co-operation among ethnic minority workers themselves.

More dialogue within and between the minority communities is vital. It cannot in any way be unusual for communities to have among them a range of attitudes and interests, sometimes apparently contradictory in nature. However, when important aspects of people's welfare are at stake, then there must be some urgency for them to work for a degree of consensus, if only to help those in the larger community to understand their needs more immediately. The communities of Indian, Pakistani and Chinese origin can sometimes be at variance, even within themselves, on issues relating to politics, religion, class and gender. While this is perfectly normal in any society, in this particular case differences are abnormally heightened, as though spotlighted by the general community. Both Indian and Chinese communities, for example, have three or four associations representing them. There has been jealousy and rivalry, especially over resources. In Newcastle upon Tyne, the allocation of resources has sometimes been delayed because the authorities expect each community to have one unified representative body. Moreover, it is obvious that racial prejudice is as alive and well within the ethnic minority communities as it is anywhere else. In this case, it can create a perfect scenario for those in power who may play at 'divide and rule'. Being constantly under a harsh spotlight places pressure on ethnic minorities as a group to be more open to debate of the issues which impede their welfare. One example is women's issues. A recently established black women's group, 'Saheli', in Newcastle, does not enjoy the approval and support it must have if it is to carry out its important role in looking to the needs of ethnic minority women. There is a danger that a counterproductive polarization results. Out of this can come adverse publicity by the media like that in a Channel 4 programme, *A Fearful Silence* (23 August 1986). Although no doubt well-intentioned, a totally negative view of Asian family life was implied by it.

A lack of dialogue and co-operation also impedes the task of organizing to counter the shared challenges of discrimination and racial harassment. With regard to the latter, national statistics indicate that there is currently a sharp increase, yet most people continue to suffer incidents helplessly. There has been no campaign organized by the police in the area, for instance, to curb or take action against racial harassment. Even if all incidents were reported, the severely overstretched service could not possible deal with them. They probably rank as the lowest in any prioritizing of offences. Northumbria Police have a system of monitoring racial incidents, but often such incidents can be open to biased interpretation. That having been said, it must be admitted that the race relations section of the service are on good terms with the CRC and they frequently liaise. What seems to be in short supply is an awareness and sensitivity among those who actually provide the service from day to day. Schools have been asked to monitor racial incidents. Once again, interpretations vary and this discredits the exercise.

Communication

There is no doubt that effective communication is required to bridge the gaps. (Newcastle Radio has started a programme, *Bridge the*

Gap, Thursdays 6.30–7.00 p.m., to help to do this.) For ethnic minorities to be able to communicate in English is something that is unlikely to lose its relevance, despite the demands recently being expressed for 'mother tongue' maintenance. The demand for E2L for adults is likely to exist for some time yet, more so if improvements are made to the way it is serviced at present. As has been pointed out by critics, E2L both in schools and for schools is poorly funded and has a low status (Bhanot, 1984; Evans, 1985). The adult sector depends to a very large extent on volunteer and hourly paid workers, and training is inadequate. Besides, as argued in the National Association for Teaching English as a Second Language to Adults report, 'serious rethinking of the principles and practice of E2L pedagogy' is required. Provision has to become more 'client-based' if it is to be relevant and at all successful. The emphasis in teaching should fall on students' practical needs in communication and be closely linked to their interests and aspirations. Linked-skill and bilingual approaches are finding favour among them. Providers will have to adapt – or risk losing interest.

In Newcastle upon Tyne, a home tuition scheme, run by both the authority and the CRC, provides volunteer tutors to teach English to adults in their homes. Although the questionable use of unpaid work is perpetuated by the scheme, there is a growing response to it both from would-be tutors and students. Teaching and learning English can be frustrating work, but there is evidence that progress in communication is made. Above all, people have a unique opportunity to make contact across the usual barriers of language and culture, and to develop valuable friendships. Already there is evidence of tutors being among the many now becoming interested in learning an Asian language. Monolingualism could eventually be outmoded. Success is also seen now and then in terms of a woman progressing from home tuition to college. A group of Bangladeshi women have joined the Royal Society of Arts' Practical Communications Profile class. (The significance of this leap from a village in Sylhet to a RSA Certificate class in Newcastle is not easy for most of us here to appreciate fully.)

Adult education providers are beginning to take a closer look at what is on offer to ethnic minorities. At the moment, a majority of classes, like wine-making and cake decoration, do not readily appeal. The Arts Council funds a multicultural arts group which meets at schools in the West End of the City. People can choose to do some of their traditional crafts in an atmosphere of sharing. English is the main, but not exclusive, language of communication. Perhaps the vital skills of communication are best picked up in neutral settings.

The school environment has been the most practical one in which ethnic minority parents can be involved in extending their communication and involvement. However, this requires a school staff who can go out of their way to be especially welcoming and supportive of ethnic minority parents. Also any link that can be forged between the school and the parents is bound to be of value to the child's learning and general welfare. Establishing these links with ethnic minority parents is a matter of priority, particularly because there is usually a great dislocation between an ethnic minority child's home and school environments, and this somehow needs bridging. This probably forms the most important aspect of a section 11 teacher's work. It seems essential that the teacher is able to communicate directly and establish an immediate rapport with an ethnic minority parent. This is likely to happen if more section 11 posts were filled from the communities themselves.

Moreover, as parents begin to play their role in school the whole effort towards anti-racist/multicultural education moves forward. Perhaps all the sophisticated policy documents, conferences and meetings can be forgotten as soon as action takes over at the grassroots? The lead for this is most likely to come from the schools with ethnic minority intake. In Westgate Hill Infants, for example, the headteacher involved parents with their children in putting together a series of readers in their various first languages. These are now being published by the city's library service and will be available at all public library service points and in schools. It is through this kind of working contact with parents that staff have the opportunity to come by what the headteacher in this school called 'a deeper understanding'.

However, spreading this understanding to the vast majority of 'all-white' schools in the region is the central challenge. A start has clearly been made in the region and movement is apparent. A headteacher summed up the current state of play as follows: 'But I'm not sure that in every situation we can possibly get commitment because people haven't been through the fire ... We still have a tremendously long way to go – but I think I see it shifting slightly.'

It is left to be seen to what extent the shift will be made and the direction it takes. There are major political, social and cultural obstacles after all. In the final analysis, what is entailed is a shift in the positions of power. Those who occupy them at present are unlikely to tolerate any destabilization of the current system. If it is a system where class inequality is one of the pillars upon which power and privilege rest, then the parallel structures that disadvantage racial minorities have little chance of being dismantled in a hurry. To leave these structures alone would surely be unwise. Yet it can make sense for minorities to shift to some extent when pressure mounts, to adopt suitable rhetoric, even become infatuated by it, and continue working in good faith for 'a good cause'. But the shift is made with blinkers hiding the unthinkable – that the system as a whole could be fundamentally inequitable. And those black people who crack the codes and are allowed in – to manage their communities (persons sitting on boards and committees, owners of large businesses) – all too often wear the same blinkers. Under such circumstances there seems little hope of significant change for the disadvantaged. Their options for action within the system remain dangerously narrow.

Notes

1. The term 'black' refers to those people who. according to the myth-ridden concepts and terminology of 'race', might fall into the category 'of non-European descent'. Obviously there is no scientific basis for such categories. To have to indicate them manifests the dilemma with terminology that occurs in 'race'-related work. Like all the terminology of 'race', 'black' is unsatisfactory. It is imprecise as a description of skin colours in a literal sense, and there are many people at present classed in this category who object to it as a proper label for themselves. They may fail to see its use as a political term to refer to all who face racism in a predominantly white society. Moreover, the term has the effect of blurring important ethnic distinctions and creates the counterproductive impression that 'black' people are a homogeneous group. However, for present purposes,

particularly in an arena in which white racism targets those who are not white, the term 'black' will remain useful in discourse.
2. The Council has not after all provided in its 1986–87 budget for these posts, although they were to be funded from section 11.
3. See, for example, North-East Chinese Association Annual Report, 1984–85.

References

ADAMSON, S., BIOTT, C., LYNCH, J., and ROBERTSON, W. (1985). 'Beyond the policy threshold'. In: CARTER, A. (Ed) *Teachers for a Multicultural Society*. London: Longman.

BHANOT, R. (1984). 'Seconds away', *Times Educational Supplement*, 19 October.

BIOTT, C., ROBERTSON, W. and LYNCH, J. (1983). *Beyond the Policy Threshold: Living with Dilemmas and Negotiating Principles for Action*. Working Paper, Sunderland Polytechnic, Faculty of Education.

CAREY, S. (1984). 'The Geordie Arabs', *New Society*, 213, May 10.

EVANS, E. (1985). *Research Project into Training of Teachers of English as a Second Language in the Post-16 Sector*. London: NATESLA.

MULLARD, C. (1984). *Anti-Racist Education: the Three Os*. Cardiff: NAME.

NEWCASTLE UPON TYNE, CITY OF. (1984). *The Council and Racial Equality: Policy Statement and Action Plan*.

NEWCASTLE UPON TYNE COMMUNITY RELATIONS COUNCIL (1986). *Good Education in a Multicultural Society*. Newcastle upon Tyne: CRC.

NG, R. (1986). 'My people: the Chinese community in the north-east', *Multicultural Teaching*, 4, 3.

QURESHI, G.D. (1986). 'The Newcastle Mosque and Muslim Community Centre', *Multicultural Teaching*, 4, 3 (Summer).

SAMRA, S.K. (1986). 'Section 11 teaching: a new ball game', *Multicultural Teaching*, 4, 3 (Summer).

SEKHRI, M (1985). *Adult education needs of the ethnic minorities*. Unpublished paper, Newcastle upon Tyne LEA.

SHAH, N. (1986). 'A black perspective on current initiatives in the north-east', *Multicultural Teaching*, 4, 3.

SISTERSON, D. and MOORE, S. (1986). 'Anti-racist teacher education network', *Multicultural Teaching*, 4, 3.

SWANN REPORT. GREAT BRITAIN. DEPARTMENT OF EDUCATION AND SCIENCE (1985). *Committee of Inquiry into the Education of Children from Ethnic Minority Groups. Education for All*, Cmnd 9453. London: HMSO.

TROYNA, B. and WILLIAMS, J. (1986). *Racism, Education and the State*. London: Croom Helm.

WALKER, J. (1986). 'SCAFRO', *Multicultural Teaching*, 4, 3.

9 Action Research as a Medium for Curriculum Development in Multicultural Education

Patricia Keel

The paper by Wendy Robertson outlines the prominent place action research occupies, as a mode of research, in the work being done in the Faculty of Education at Sunderland Polytechnic. An example of this work is the project, carried out between spring 1984 and summer 1985, supporting teachers' initiatives in multicultural education (Biott, Robertson and Lynch, 1983) in two primary schools in north-east England.

This paper outlines how the project was planned and initiated. It briefly reviews action taken, and then discusses issues that emerged from analysis of data. It finally explores resulting implications for the kind of action research that may be carried out in schools to promote good practice in education for a multi-ethnic society.

Setting up the Project

A junior school (school A) and an infant school (school B) were selected for the project. Both schools are in an area close to where shipbuilding and associated industries have traditionally provided work, but where there is considerable unemployment now. The community in school A's catchment has tended to retain its traditional character, and still has a strong sense of cultural identity. The school population is almost completely ethnically homogeneous. School B, on the other hand, serves a community less traditionally based in the area. Many people are professionals who have moved into the area, attracted by the housing, and among them are ethnic minority families. The school's population reflects this in its 14 per cent of ethnic minority children.

In response to factors described in the preceding paper on multicultural education development in an area of the north-east, this local education authority was the first in the region to formulate policy on multicultural education, and quickly followed through with an in-service Education for Teachers' programme. At the same time, Sunderland Polytechnic had conceived of this project following previous research (Biott, Robertson and Lynch, 1983). The timing was right with regard to the sequence of developments in the particular LEA. There was immediate interest in the project, followed by full co-operation from the LEA and the school's headteachers in setting it up.

The project was planned around a number of concepts in action research. Collaboration with teachers was to be the keynote. An action research model (Halsey, 1972) was followed in identifying areas in current practice suitable for innovation. Aims and principles of procedure were defined and plans devised for action. Interview was the main research tool (Simons, 1981). Data includes audio tapes of interviews with teachers and children, of staff meetings, of teaching and learning activities, and transcripts of these. There are communication documents, fieldnotes, teachers' notes, children's work and other relevant materials. These constitute a case record (Stenhouse, 1978) to accompany the final report. Data has been analysed by means of a progressive focusing technique suggested in Winter's (1982) system of dilemma analysis. Analysis and evaluation is intended as 'illuminative' (Parlett and Hamilton, 1972).

During the project both schools shared a number of experiences. There was, for example, the teachers' industrial action throughout the period. As might be expected, this factor probably considerably influenced the degree of interest teachers took in the project and the time they were able to give to it. Talk in staffrooms was frequently dominated by the action and the saga of developments. For both schools it posed acute dilemmas, especially with regard to developments of community involvement, which obviously had to be curtailed. On numerous occasions staff were heard expressing misgivings over the damage being done to relations between parents and themselves. At a time when local authorities across the country were wielding an axe on finances, both schools suffered staff reductions. The pinch was evident in the extra pressure on time felt by teachers. Resources too were being increasingly curtailed.

At the same time, the LEA made fresh demands on schools. A response to the authority's policy on racial equality was required from every school, including its board of governors. This was just one among several other required responses. There were calls for emphasis on mathematics, science, computers, special needs and closer links with the community. Thus although this LEA may be seen to have spearheaded movement in schools towards multicultural education by producing a clear anti-racist policy (City of Newcastle, 1984) to which schools had to respond with a written school policy, it would seem that many schools were yet to respond in action. Anti-racist/multicultural education may not have ranked high in their list of priorities. In the two schools in question it was evident that for a majority of staff it did not rank high, in spite of the presence of this project, and the intended 'whole-school-approach to it.

It is worth reflecting on the dynamics of institutional response to the various demands, especially those for change. Among the various demands schools currently face many involve making changes in educational perspectives. Although demand for change can come from within an organization or institution, often such demands come from outside and the responses organizations make are not always straightforward. Generally they do not make dramatic, overnight changes (March, 1981). Change is more prosaic, often the result of 'adaptive behaviour' which may include resisting change in a confusing world. The survival of the organization is the more compelling requirement in the long term. Teachers and the school have to keep going. They respond to the varying demands made on them at any one time with a kind of long-suffering good-nature, without absolute panic, because they know from experience there will be ways to ride with the tide.

Initiating the Project

To ensure that a 'whole-school' approach might be adopted, all members of the teaching staff in both schools were asked to attend meetings initially to discuss the project and to arrive at plans.

Thereafter, there were staff meetings at which reports on the work were made occasionally. However, although over the period more teachers became involved than there were at the beginning, there was a significant number who did not become involved, several expressedly because they had no time or because this would not fit with the teaching they were doing at the time. The factors earlier discussed – the industrial action and extra pressure, from staffing cuts and other competing educational priorities – could have been contributory reasons.

Another factor, not always clearly articulated, may have been a resistance particularly to the kind of change which multicultural education appeared to demand. From the outset, the researcher emphasized the principle of racial equality as being at the core of multicultural education. It needed to be clear that the *raison d'etre* of multicultural education lies in the injustices within society, and distortions and imbalances within education, brought about by prejudice and racism. The inner city disturbances of recent years are accepted by many as evidence of a deeply felt sense of racial injustice. People of that point of view tend also to believe that education needs to address itself to combating racism. However, for a large number of teachers it would appear that education and 'politics' must be kept separate. To them, riots and social unrest are to do with 'politics' – problems for politicians. They see themselves as educators, and as such, they feel they must preserve a political neutrality, and resist demands made on them to take political stances. They appear to link multicultural education with politics of the 'left' – with 'black trouble-makers'. This is not surprising when the popular media have consistently created this impression in their presentation of such items as the Honeyford affair and the Swann Report. It was evident from contact with teachers in both schools A and B that there was a distrust of the. underlying 'politics' of multicultural education. Moreover, it was noticeable that those who readily took on the principles of multicultural education, including its anti-racist core, tended to be those who might be described as being less conservative, and more inclined towards notions of political and social change that might bring about greater justice and equality across boundaries of sex, class and ethnicity. They were very likely to see parallel lines of discrimination and injustice running through these categories. Other individuals may be similarly aware. However, there seems to be a schism in attitudes, with the predominant group believing that there is little to be done to change 'the *real* world' – and that the world is well known for its 'I'm alright Jacks'.

Thus although a few teachers were already disposed to thinking and talking about issues to do with with race, many appeared distinctly uncomfortable. For most of them the whole field of race and its confusing vocabulary were daunting and preferably to be avoided. As the researcher herself is black, it is difficult to judge to what extent the discomfort was exacerbated because there is in fact some evidence to the contrary. Some teachers took this opportunity to explore a black point of view.

The researcher's role was naturally a problematic one. It was not easy, without prior experience, always to judge the right approach. Tact and sensitivity were required, but also openness and frankness. Here was an outsider, coming in from an institution thought of as representing 'experts'. She claimed she was no expert – she was here to collaborate with teachers on strategies for implementing multicultural education in the classroom. But what is multicultural education? And why all the emphasis on 'race'? It was obvious from the outset that it would take a long time to gain trust and confidence on both sides, and to get beyond the polite formality of the newly acquainted. By the end, it was possible to achieve this with only a minority of the staffs, to drop one's guard and openly to debate the issues in what after all is a thorny field.

Action Taken

Audio-taped interviews with teachers began in the spring of 1984. Both parties in these interviews found it difficult to come to terms with the tape recorder. For the researcher, this was in the initial phases because of a lack of experience; for several teachers, it was because of an initial shyness, which in some cases merged with a mistrust over how the tapes might subsequently be used. This was in spite of the agreement with teachers that they would have the right to refuse clearance for the use of transcript data. There was a request, for example, for a recording of a staff meeting to be scrubbed, and this was complied with. Not every teacher agreed to be interviewed. Some politely, but consistently, avoided any involvement.

Following the first interviews, it was possible to start planning with interested teachers various teaching strategies they might try out. A format for planning and note-taking by teachers was devised in order to have adequate records of each 'experiment', particularly for the purpose of analysis and evaluation. It was necessary to keep in close contact with teachers, discussing possibilities, planning, monitoring action and evaluating. But there was never enough time, and discussions tended to be snatched during breaks or at best after school when people were tired and thinking of getting home. Headteachers did try on occasions to relieve a teacher in class, so that s/he might be interviewed uninterrupted.

Most of the activities recorded were based in very ordinary curriculum activities, e.g. story telling with discussion, discussing pictures, games, television programmes, assemblies, music, cooking, etc. A particular story or picture was chosen for the elements in it thought suitable for multicultural education. Later the activity was analysed in relation to objectives previously set, and evaluated. When transcripts of recordings could be made, a greater depth of analysis was possible and a greater increase in awareness usually followed.

There were some larger-scale projects. For example, in school B, children visited four ethnically different kitchens in homes of some of their schoolmates. They had the chance to see similarities and differences, and make a first acquaintance with much that was new for them. In school A where the term's classwork was arranged around a chosen topic in one class, several weeks were given to a study of so-called 'gypsies'. This coincided with the Romany Fair on the town's moor, and it was hoped to explore prejudice via this topic. However, the larger projects were not always easy to organize and keep track of, and a measure of successful consciousness raising more often comes out of the use of a simple 15-minute story and discussion, recorded and more readily analysed. There is the example of a teacher who told Joan Solomon's *Kate's Party* to a group of children. She discovered that she did not know what a yam is, and that she would need to find that out to tell the story more successfully. She also found herself implying during discussion a preference for silky blonde hair as opposed to that of the little black girl in the story, because her hair, the book said, pulled and hurt when her mother combed it for the party. In another instance when some pictures featuring people of different ethnic background in Britain were discussed in class, the teacher was later somewhat dismayed at having assumed that the black woman in the picture was from Africa.

The 'post mortem' discussions with teachers were recorded wherever possible. They form a valuable part of the data collection. The following section explores some of the major issues drawn from an analysis of transcripts of interviews and discussions. As agreed with teachers, quotations from transcripts used here remain anonymous.

Emerging Issues: 'All-white' Notion

In recent years it has been evident (Biott, Robertson and Lynch, 1983) that a large percentage of teachers in predominantly white schools in the region would have said: 'We don't need to do anything – we don't have that problem here.' It is probably an indication of teachers' earlier concepts of multicultural education that when interviewed in spring 1984, several equated multicultural education with special provision for ethnic minority children and talked about the 'problem' of having them in their classrooms; more recent evidence shows that some teachers still apparently think in these terms (Troyna and Ball, 1985).

Nowadays teachers aware of multicultural education are likely to refer to the fact that they only have one or two ethnic minority children in school as a lack of a starting-point for multicultural education: 'with society changing there was an up and coming need ...though in some ways it may be difficult because there's such a low ethnic intake in the school.'

Multicultural Education 'Talk'

Because of the Newcastle upon Tyne Authority's programme for schools to implement multicultural education, teachers have become familiar with the jargon and rhetoric of multicultural education and several now talk fluently about the 'need' in terms of 'society changing' and also about how, given time, multicultural education *ought* to be in practice:

I think we're really aiming at bringing about an awareness of the different cultures in all our children, therefore ...and perhaps even more important... in areas where there are no minority children to provide this sort of thing, because it may be more difficult later to bring about an awareness.

It's the changing of people's thought patterns... putting wider lenses on a camera, so to speak, trying to broaden their thoughts.

It's just using things that crop up in the day ...I don't believe in putting up a chart of things...it's not a geography lesson where you're going to put up a map ... [It's] spontaneous questions and honest answers ... an Eskimo doesn't live in an igloo anymore ... Where does the Eskimo live? He's got a house. It's as simple as that.

But I don't agree with forcing it down children in a parrot-fashion sense... celebrating Chinese New Year, celebrating *every* event... doing a topic because it's multicultural education and it's trendy to do it... I don't think that's right.

I think it's important that our children in the school are made aware of other people, other people's religious beliefs... other people's customs, festivals, because we don't have a big variety, and if you want them to become more tolerant in the wider community, perhaps they move to another area of the city or perhaps another city, you want them to have come across these different, well, different kinds of people, perhaps from different countries, from different backgrounds... and I think it is important that our children should become more aware.

We're broadening out the curriculum, we're beginning to think that little bit further out than we did before, and it's bringing a richness into what we're doing that wasn't there before – an added dimension.

Multicultural education... has to be an integral part of the curriculum, having a programme dotted here and dotted there, or a lesson dotted here and dotted there, is not the way to go about it.

Teachers here illustrate their goodwill towards some of the principles of multicultural education. There is even a vision of its 'integral part' in the curriculum. It is worth looking closely at the concepts embedded in these remarks. First, there is the idea of 'broadening', 'an added dimension' and a new 'richness', and this is applied both to 'the curriculum' and to 'awareness' or 'thought patterns', especially those of children. There is also the realization that there is a particular need in areas 'where there are no minority children'. An acceptance that change is a necessary part of the process of multicultural education is implied if not stated. There is a wish to avoid tokenism – celebrating Chinese New Year because it is 'trendy'. There is a suggestion that there are 'spontaneous questions' from children which need 'honest' and accurate answers. Most of these remarks are in terms of bringing about awareness of 'other' people's cultures, people 'from different countries' – the 'Eskimo', for instance. There is no talk of becoming aware of our own cultures, our own attitudes and prejudices, least of all of racism and the injustices it creates in society.

Race and its Terminology

The discomfort that the issue of race produced was evident frequently. Here teachers seemed most vulnerable in their lack of expertise when venturing into this sensitive field. In predominantly white areas, there is less familiarity with the issue of race and its terminology than there might be in ethnically mixed areas. There is much less sophistication in the adoption of more current terminology. For example, although the term 'coloured' has been out of favour for some time now (Gaine, 1984) a majority of people in this region still find difficulty in using the terms 'black' or 'ethnic minority'. There is usually a sense of embarrassment and reluctance if and when conversation turns towards the ethnic minorities. There is frequent confusion over the terms Asian, Indian, Pakistani, Chinese, West Indian, and so on:

> I think I have thirteen minority culture children – one Chinese and the rest Asian.

> We have obviously more of the ethnic minority here, whereas the last school I had one child, who was a half-caste Indian... whereas

here it is quite nice because we do get the mix. I haven't had any Chinese children but there are the odd ones in the school. We had a little Negro girl... but basically it seems to be the Indians loosely, because I know some of them are from Pakistan ... or are the majority from Pakistan?

. . . we don't have very many children in this school who are coloured.

If teachers had the time and opportunity to be exposed to material dealing with racial issues and to discuss these more frequently than they are probably inclined to at present, then they might feel less ill at ease and much more confident.

Negative Racial Attitudes

Yet there was little doubt that teachers did, however vaguely, link multicultural education with race. A few, even at the earliest contact, saw negative racial attitudes in children, at any rate, as a good reason for considering multicultural education: 'now I have noticed that I have one or two 'yukky' little white children, not in every other situation, but they laugh at the ethnic minorities.' On the other hand, most teachers appeared not to have considered anything they might do to reduce prejudice: 'Reducing prejudice? It's rather difficult... I've never really thought about it before.'

Likewise, several teachers were defensive about children's attitudes. It was often asserted that children do not notice racial differences:

I don't know really, in the nursery I am very loath to point out differences that they haven't noticed.

... they haven't really looked in detail at people's features and colour, outside really Europeans, because we don't have very many children in this school who are coloured.

Quite a lot of the photographs were of people in India, and the children were much more fascinated by the costumes and the articles in the shops, the kinds of buildings, than they were particularly in the appearance of the people.

In these instances there seemed a willingness to apply a blanket assumption that young children do not of their own accord notice racial differences. Yet there is ample evidence to the contrary (Milner, 1983; Davey, 1980).

Often, however, the blame for negative racial attitudes in children was firmly placed at the door of parents or their background:

> Actually it showed me how prejudiced some of them really were and obviously the prejudices come from home. What they hear at home comes out in what they say in the classroom.

> You couldn't say that these children are very racist... not knowingly... but at the same time, in their attitude there was something that made me very, very uneasy. Some lack of tolerance... and it also became obvious that that had come from the home.

School's Role in Racial Incidents

While it may be thought the children's racial prejudice comes from their background, there seemed a general lack of conviction among teachers about what the school can do about it. It became clear that negative racial attitudes of parents within the school's community were regarded as a serious constraint to multicultural education initiatives:

> But I think this school with it being such a small proportion of minority children... you have to be careful not to annoy parents by stressing multicultural education too much.

> But as I said before, we mustn't go overboard... to appear to be doing more for the ethnic minority children.

> ... it [multicultural education] raises quite intense feelings in people as well as being a very sort of emotive issue, so you've got to be careful really I think.

There was evidence of some parents querying multicultural

initiatives. At a meeting with some parents who form the 'Friends' group in one school, there were underlying signs of disquiet expressed in conversation. The headteacher was constantly aware of the sensitive task of 'gradually changing' negative attitudes of some parents. Nor was there a strong commitment in the schools to curb racial remarks, for instance,. Many saw name-calling as a natural part of children's behaviour, and assumed racial name-calling was no different: 'and when children are young they shout names at each other, whatever it is ... when a child wears glasses, someone is unkind and calls them "Four Eyes" or something... so this is what I feel, there's not a lot you can do about calling names. It's often done between friends, isn't it?'. And another teacher talking about children's use of language during a unit on people's skin colour: 'at first, in a way, it was a little bit unacceptable because they took the words and phrases that they'd heard initially perhaps as abuse, they didn't realize it was abuse.'

Stereotypical Images

Yet several said that the children's attitudes to other races left a lot to be desired and that it was children's stereotypical images that needed changing. A teacher discussing the BBC programme *Zig-Zag* said:

> ...the programme today is the modern Eskimo, the modern Innuit which will surprise the children even more because the children's idea of an Eskimo, or Innuit, is the old igloo, snow-shoes, a spear in their hand, which of course is not so. And they'll discover today, they're making timber and corrugated iron... they have their own towns and communities and supermarkets, and they don't have cars but they have the equivalent of a car, these snow mobile things.

One may speculate here on the extent of teachers' own stereotypical notions, and middle-class, Western standards need equal consideration. Instead, however, the media are seen to be responsible for children's stereotypical images:

> ... South Africa at the moment is a prime example. See you take

a seven to 11-year-old, which is the children we're dealing with in this school. How many will say 'Those poor people are being driven from their homes?' They don't know the background to it. All they see is police or the army or whatever it is keeping law and order and a lot of children might think, 'Oh, those blacks are causing trouble again'.

Once again, it needs to be borne in mind, that it is not just children who are subject to media stereotyping and political bias, but the great majority of us. Moreover, there is the difficulty that any new information offered by the content of multicultural education must always penetrate a filter of stereotypical images and preconceived notions, thus militating against any change in perspectives and attitudes. There have to be effective ways in multicultural education of liberating thought processes from their dependence on stereotypical and ethnocentric perspectives. Children need fresh patterns for thinking and assessing the world around them. This demand should be the main concern in multicultural education rather than cramming into the curriculum all sorts of exotic content.

Multicultural Education Content

Yet an emphasis has been placed not only by teachers, but by many in the field of multicultural education, on the *content* that might be appropriate for multicultural education in the classroom. More often than not, appropriate content is seen in terms of subject areas:

> ... we've been discussing the idea of bringing in multicultural and multi-ethnic aspects to the religious curriculum... things like festivals, food, this kind of thing.

> ...I'd be interested in doing something where we took different countries of the world and look at their festivals and their food.

> You know you've got Geography, you've got awareness of the globe, the world ...history, religion, culture, foods, dress, homes, houses.

Often there is a sense of remoteness that teachers seem to feel from much of the material currently associated with multicultural education. They often use the term 'foreign' in talking about such material: 'In fact they [the class] didn't comment on the fact that the children [in the story] were foreign at all... but they were very interested to know where they came from.' This notion of foreignness links with the fact that multicultural education is, in some schools of thought, considered best approached through the subject area of Geography. There seems a willingness, even in teachers who may be set against multicultural education, to teach about other countries and peoples ('after all, haven't we always done this?') especially if they can remain remote and foreign, as they have remained in Geography.

It is when the material comes closer to home – to do with the peoples and cultures within the UK – that teachers feel more doubtful, frequently citing their lack of 'first-hand experience': ' I think a visit to temples or to have someone who really knows about it – I don't really know enough about it to have a lot of confidence.' Expressed here is the insecurity teachers experience in this context. They feel expected suddenly to have at their fingertips a vast encyclopaedic knowledge of all cultures, which their own education certainly did not give them: 'I think one reason why perhaps some teachers don't go into things is that they don't really know ... Ignorance... and you know another side of it is that people don't always feel confident that they have the policy clearly enough in their mind to know what they're trying to do.' They can find themselves in an extremely vulnerable position often without expecting it. A teacher picks up one of the growing collection of the new multicultural books for children at story-time. She says later: 'I think I could have gone into what yams were... I could have done it if it had been something like an avocado pear, but I couldn't describe a yam because I don't know what yams look like or what they taste like.'

It is not surprising, then, if teachers turn with hope to packaged material; the more convenient the pack is, the better:

... the way the Durham teachers have done this... I mean I could use this completely down to the worksheets, the questions.

... even if the BBC or ITV didn't do this, colleges or institutions of education... could do packs. I think really you could list the major religions of the world and do a pack on that. And you could go through all the major races of the world.

Another teacher, just completing a package, said: 'Now that I've done that... I don't know what to do next, I mean, it seems so good, it seems such a shame that there isn't more material about, because without this I couldn't have done it.' It seems that if the BBC or ITV would take on the awkward job, then one may never need to oneself, because problems of content and even pedagogy would rest with the producers of packs, along with other considerations such as the unpleasant issues to do with race.

How Will Children Cope?

If all this new content is mind-boggling for teachers, then it is not surprising if they think that the children will be out of their depth. Primary school pedagogy is rooted in the principles of basing learning on the child's immediate experience. Teachers, therefore, often express unease over how children are going to take in what would seem remote and foreign to their experience:

> But the other thing I thought about, with the Chinese New Year celebrations in the hall, was that very young children like nursery age children find it very hard to be involved ... it was lovely, we all enjoyed watching the dragon... but find it very hard to understand, and the experiences which like New Year, even in this country, which is lovely, but as long as you realize that with very young children, what's so far out of the experience...

And again:

> It's no good someone [a child] living in [this] district... hearing about... kids in Birmingham, kids in one of the townships of Johannesburg, because some of them will listen to it, but others, they'll just think 'Well, what's that... I don't even know about London. I've never been to London. I don't know what a London child does in the East End or wherever they live.'

While it is fair to question whether a three-year-old can cope with the notion of a New Year, nevertheless it is assumed generally in infant schools that children will benefit pedagogically from the celebration in school of birthdays and the rather more complex celebrations of Christmas and Easter. Likewise, although the acquisition of spatial concepts by children has to be borne in mind when material to do with geographically distant places is presented, we nevertheless frequently compromise on this consideration. It becomes a question of when such compromises are going to be worthwhile, and also on who decides and on whose behalf. A nursery nurse aptly pointed out:

> I think the materials should be aimed at all different classes and cultures. I know when I was at school we had stories – Janet and John go out in the car – and the majority in my class didn't have cars; you know it was just like a fairy tale. We couldn't relate that to our lives at all.

Pedagogical Processes in Multicultural Education

What seems essential is that teachers have the opportunity consciously to explore these pedagogical issues within the context of multicultural education. In this project, this did occur to some extent at least. Some teachers became aware that multicultural education is not solely about injecting new content into the curriculum, and that to assume this could be counterproductive. As Ashriff points out:

> Often the descriptive mode of multicultural education succeeds only in reinforcing prejudices prevalent among students. The Victorian intellectuals were well enough versed in other cultures, but this did not dispel this racism. I would submit that multicultural education today is Victorian in outlook, and the present obsession of teachers with content, will produce a more knowledgeable, but no less a racist society. (Ashriff, 1985, p.14)

These teachers, therefore, avoided tokenistic content, and concentrated instead on material seeking to sensitize children to principles of justice, consideration for fellow human beings, open-mindedness and co-operation. One teacher experimented with an unsupervised co-operative musical activity, recording the children's talk while they were on their own (Biott, Robertson and Lynch, 1983; Sharan, 1980). It appears from the transcripts that the spirit of competition and 'one-upmanship' is learned early in life.

Another revelation was how unused to freedom from the teacher's supervision and authority the children seemed. After a few minutes of horseplay, when their 'co-operative' activity had degenerated, they decided on their own initiative to go and seek out their teacher! This suggests that we may be some way off from achieving what Alan James sees as the aim in education:

> to enable all children to achieve autonomy, and this includes independence from their own 'roots': they should be able to look at the ideas and work of any human being and judge them on their own merits, irrespective of the skin colour, cultural background or socio-historical location of their maker – to identify themselves with other human beings as fellow-workers with a common interest in ending exploitation and injustice based on race, sex or way of life. (James and Jeffcoate, 1981, p.28)

Raising Awareness

It is only as a result of teachers' recorded experimentation which they have monitored, analysed and evaluated, that they move on to other levels of awareness and questioning. Here is what some of them said:

> ... the only danger is that we're spreading it too thinly... you've got to be careful that this is not treated as very superficial, that whatever you do, you do in some sort of depth.

> ... afterwards a couple of kids said, 'Oh, miss, can we do some more?' So there is interest there and I think it's something that can be built on.

> Now if I was to do that sort of topic again, then I would most certainly include that book.

... lots of interesting facts and discussion.

... they used very good vocabulary which they haven't used before ... so it was very useful from a creative point of view.

It seemed, moreover, that just around the corner, despite the challenges, was the possibility of a new excitement with education and a sense of personal discovery:

I certainly wouldn't be put off because to me it *is* important... from my point of view. I want to know.

But it's helped me keep up with, so that I can know the truth about life in China and it's washed away all of the myths that I might have thought were true.

Perhaps it is most significant when thoughts such as the following emerge:

You can have every bit of resource imaginable ...film, books, pamphlets, everything, visitors... and if a teacher has an attitude, I've got to say, anti... you know, a racialist attitude, inborn or just the way they feel, or opinion they have, you're batting on a losing wicket.

... a lot of people do feel that they've grown up in a society where colour isn't either talked about or it's not very nice or whatever and all their lives they've grown up with this... I think it's difficult, people have got to ... to get over this way we've grown up in ... and start talking about it in a positive way, rather than ignoring it in a negative one possibly. But that's easier said than done, probably.

Implications

Action Research as a Tool

Judging, then, from the path towards awareness taken by at least some teachers it can be argued that action research offers a useful medium for achieving the particular nature of curriculum change required for implementing genuine multicultural education. Far more complex changes are involved in this case than, say, introducing a newer approach in Mathematics, although curriculum changes in that subject have been difficult enough.

Taking multicultural education on board presupposes a fresh look not only at basic principles enshrined in education, but also at how these are linked to basic moral and social principles of democracy and justice held in our society. Therefore, a process which delicately tunes teachers into a set of attitudes based on these principles lies at the heart of good multicultural practice. This tuning-in cannot take place by decree, and this is borne out by ample evidence suggesting that policy documents do not necessarily translate into classroom practice (Troyna and Ball, 1985). This is not to say that policy documents are not important, but they may indeed not be worth the paper they are written on without an accompanying process by which teachers are sensitized to the issues involved. These issues have a good chance of coming alive for teachers through a form of action research in the context of their daily work. Awareness then comes from within each teacher's experience, in her/his professional role, rather than from cold, external authority.

The Framework Needed

But how are teachers to become engaged in action research? There are numerous examples of teachers who have become so engaged (e.g. Adelman, 1983), but is it possible to engage more of them? It may be possible within a given framework.

A first step is for an LEA to have a policy that spells out unambiguously for all in the service the principles underlying its adoption, and what is expected by way of action. Although it only represents the voice of external authority, a policy document both provides legitimacy and offers a stimulus.

The next vital step is for the LEA to ensure appropriate INSET. (The parallel need for appropriate initial teacher training cannot be too strongly emphasized.) In-service courses should tackle a clarification of the educational, social and moral principles underlying multicultural education (Dunn, 1986). It is evident from this research project that most teachers are confused and even suspicious about why multicultural education is being promoted. In looking at the social and moral principles, courses need to present relevant material on racial prejudice, racism and injustice, and seek to equip teachers with the confidence to deal with the confusing concepts and terminology in the field, and to debate its issues openly. Only in this way can they have the competence to do likewise in the classroom. In looking at the pedagogical processes fundamental to multicultural education, teachers may be directed to the kind of thinking on the curriculum expressed recently by the DES:

> The more the curriculum includes objectives which go beyond subject matter and promote the development of particular attitudes and capabilities, the stronger are the implications for a variety and range of teaching approaches to be employed if all the objectives are to be achieved. (HMI, 1985)

Alan James spells out these approaches for multicultural education:

> Such an education can only be provided... in a context where children are encouraged to articulate their own ideas, to question, to listen to each other, to co-operate rather than compete – and as they grow, to take an increasing part in the practice of democracy – in debate and negotiation, and the election of representatives within school, and in informed and critical use of information and opinion in society. (James and Jeffcoate, 1981, p.28)

The other important element in such in-service training is equipping teachers with the basic tools for action research. Given that curriculum change needs to be well researched, who better to contribute to this research than teachers themselves? They could be encouraged to collaborate within school and perhaps across schools, to put innovatory measures to rigorous test. In groups they could look at existing curriculum against a consideration of multicultural principles and arrive at areas for possible innovation. Having specific objectives for action, they would monitor action taken, making notes, recordings, and so on, for collection of data.

They would then be in a position to analyse and evaluate the experiment. They might be offered the facility of pooling reports for a publication to be circulated in local schools and further afield.

Of course there is the question of time available for such work, and this is where authorities need to put their money if they do indeed expect teachers to take multicultural education seriously. During the project it was frequently obvious that teachers cannot be expected to produce the goods without having some time set aside for the discussion, planning and preparing that such curriculum innovation necessitates. A whole-school approach is essential if action is going to be comprehensive and consistent. Collaboration is its corner-stone. Everyone in the field is still feeling their way through a maze of complexities. If teachers are the people who must in the end deliver the goods to their young clients, then the field should be democratized, so that they might actively join in the search for what multicultural education means in the classroom.

References

ADELMAN, C. (1983) *A Fair Hearing for All*. High Wycombe: Bulmershe Institute of Higher Education.

ASHRIFF, S. (1985). 'An anti-racist in place of a multicultural education', *Educational Journal*, 6, 2.

BIOTT, C. (1983). *Getting on without the Teacher*. Occasional Paper, Sunderland Polytechnic, Faculty of Education.

BIOTT, C. and ROBERTSON, W. (1984). 'Supporting teachers' own programme towards multicultural education', *Multicultural Teaching*, 2 (Spring).

BIOTT, C., ROBERTSON, W. and LYNCH, J. (1983). *Beyond the Policy Threshold: Living with Dilemmas and Negotiating Principles for Action*. Working Paper, Sunderland Polytechnic, Faculty of Education.

DAVEY, A (1980). 'Ethnic awareness and ethnic differentiation amongst primary school children', *New Community*, 8, 51–60.

DUNN, D. (1986). 'In-service miseducation'. In: ARORA, R.K. and DUNCAN, C.G. (Eds) *Multicultural Education: Towards Good Practice*. London: Routledge and Kegan Paul.

GAINE, C. (1984). 'What do we call people?', *Multicultural Teaching*, 3, 1.

HALSEY, A.H. (1972). *Educational Priority, 1*. London: HMSO.

HER MAJESTY'S INSPECTORATE (1985). *The Curriculum from 5 to 16*. Department of Education and Science. London: HMSO.

JAMES, A. and JEFFCOATE, R. (Eds) (1981). *The School in the Multicultural Society*. London: Harper and Row.

MARCH, J.G. (1981). 'Footnotes to organisational change', *Administrative Science Quarterly*, 26, 563–77.

MILNER, D. (1983). *Children and Race: Ten Years On*. London: Ward Lock.

NEWCASTLE UPON TYNE, CITY OF (1984). *The Council and Racial Equality: Policy Statement and Action Plan*.

PARLETT, M. and HAMILTON, D. (1972). *Evaluation in Illumination: a New Approach to the study of Innovatory Programs*. CRES Paper 9. Edinburgh: University of Edinburgh.

SHARAN, S. (1980). 'Co-operative learning in small groups: recent methods and effects on achievement, attitudes and ethnic relations', *Review of Educational Research*, 50, 2, 241–71.

SIMONS, H. (1981). 'Conversation piece: the practice of interviewing in case study research.' In: ADELMAN, C. (Ed) *Uttering, Muttering*. London: Grant McIntyre.

STENHOUSE, L. (1978). 'Case study and case records: towards a contemporary history of education', *British Educational Research Journal*, 4, 2, 21–40.

TROYNA, B. and BALL, W. (1985). 'Educational decision making and issues of race: a study of policy and practice on multicultural education in a local education authority', *Quarterly Journal of Social Affairs*, 4, 1, 311–25.

WINTER, R. (1982). 'Dilemma analysis', *Cambridge Journal of Education*, 1.